hm

STUDY SKILLS PROGRAM
Level II
Revised Edition

Developed by hm: The Study Skills Group

Author and Senior Editor: David Marshak

Revision Editor: Paula Phipps

Editors: Kiyo Morimoto, *Director*
Bureau of Study Counsel
Harvard University

Jerome A. Pieh, *Headmaster*
Milton Academy

James J. McGuinn

 The National Association of Secondary School Principals
Reston, Virginia 22091

Our thanks to all of the hundreds of teachers, students, counselors, and administrators who used the first edition of the **LEVEL II PROGRAM** and contributed their suggestions to us; and particularly to five talented educators who reviewed all of the final draft with care and imagination: Eleanor T. Hall; Lynne Heckmann; John F. Miller; Pam Mueller; and Phyllis Allen Smith.

The three step study method in Unit V is loosely adapted from the SQ3R Method in *Effective Study* by Francis P. Robinson. Copyright 1941, 1946 by Harper and Row Publishers, Inc. Copyright 1961, 1970, by Francis P. Robinson. Reprinted by permission of Harper and Row, Publishers, Inc.

The passage on page 24 is excerpted from pages 458-60 of *Energy, Matter, and Change: Excursions into Physical Science* by Ronald D. Townsend. Copyright 1973 by Scott, Foresman and Co. Reprinted by permission of Scott, Foresman and Co.

The textbook passages on pages 35 and 38 are excerpted from *The Story of America* by Harold H. Eibling, Fred M. King, and James Harlow. Adapted by Milton Finkelstein. Copyright 1969 by Laidlaw Brothers. Published by Laidlaw Brothers, Division of Doubleday and Co., Inc. Reprinted by permission of Laidlaw Brothers.

© Copyright 1986 by **NATIONAL ASSOCIATION OF SECONDARY SCHOOL PRINCIPALS**, 1904 Association Drive, Reston, Virginia 22091. Scott D. Thomson, Executive Director. Thomas F. Koerner, Director of Publications. All rights reserved. Manufactured in the United States of America. All **hm** Study Skills materials are copyrighted. No portion of this publication or its accompanying materials may be reproduced or copied, or stored in any information retrieval system, without the written permission of **NASSP**.

ISBN 0-88210-099-8

ISBN 0-88210-100-5

TABLE OF CONTENTS

Introduction		1
I.	LEARNING TO LISTEN	4
II.	VOCABULARY: GETTING MEANING FROM CONTEXT	8
III.	NOTE TAKING METHODS	18
IV.	LISTENING AND TAKING NOTES	28
V.	A WAY TO READ TEXTBOOKS	33
VI.	SOLVING PROBLEMS	40
VII.	HOW DO YOU STUDY?	48
VIII.	IMPROVING YOUR MEMORY	55
IX.	ORGANIZING THE PARAGRAPH	65
X.	PREPARING FOR AND TAKING TESTS: OBJECTIVE QUESTIONS	73
XI.	PREPARING FOR AND TAKING TESTS: ESSAY QUESTIONS	85
XII.	USING YOUR TIME	93

INTRODUCTION

WHAT IS STUDYING?

Some students define studying as what you do to prepare for a test. This is only one small sense of what the word means. Studying has a much larger definition. It means learning for a purpose. Whenever you are learning for a purpose, you are studying. You might be reading a book, listening to a friend, watching a movie, doing homework, practicing a sport, or thinking by yourself. All of these activities are studying.

Try to keep this larger definition in mind as you go through this Program. It's easy to remember in this way: if you are learning for a purpose, then you are studying.

WHAT ARE STUDY SKILLS?

Study skills are skills for learning. They are methods, ways of doing things, that can help make learning easier for you. They can also help you to get more work done and to learn more in a given period of time. There are skills involved in much of what we do in life, such as playing a musical instrument, shooting a jump shot, sewing a piece of clothing, tuning an engine, baking a cake, or dancing. Study skills are skills you can master that will help you to learn more effectively.

Study skills are not a substitute for the work that learning requires. However, using these skills will help you gain more from the effort and time you devote to learning, particularly to school work.

WHAT IS THE VALUE OF STUDY SKILLS?

Many of you are probably already using at least some study skills. This Program can help you to learn other skills that will let you use your time and energy even more effectively.

If you are not doing as well in school as you'd like, you may find this Program very helpful. Many students who want to learn have difficulty in school. Often this is because they don't know how to study. The study skills that you can learn in this Program can help you to overcome some of these difficulties. They can help you improve the effectiveness of your learning. They can also help you discover that your studying can become more successful and more enjoyable.

LEARNING STYLE

Not everyone learns in the same way. In fact, people learn in many different ways. Some people learn best when they can read about something new before they try to do it. Others learn best when they can work with something new in a "hands-on" way. Still other people learn best when they can listen to new material. These are only a few of the ways in which people learn differently.

The ways in which you learn best make up your *learning style*. No ways of learning or *learning styles* are better than any others. But they are different.

EXERCISE I

Directions: What do you know about your own *learning style*? Look at the words and phrases listed below. Circle the ones that describe how you learn best. You may also write other words and phrases that describe your *learning style* on the lines below.

Remember: There are no right or wrong answers! Just think about how you learn best. You can circle and write as many words and phrases as you need to describe your learning style. You might circle some that seem like opposites. For example, you might circle both "by myself" and "with a friend," because both work well for you depending on what you are trying to learn.

watching	listening	doing
reading	thinking about	working when I have to
experimenting	writing	getting it right
learning from my mistakes	proving my point	doing something I care about
being creative	talking it over with a friend	"hands-on"
by myself	asking questions	with a group
looking things up		

_____

_____

_____

_____

LEARNING STUDY SKILLS: STUDY SKILLS AND LEARNING STYLE

People learn study skills best by doing them, that is, practicing the skills. To master a new study skill, you usually need to practice it at least three or four times, sometimes more. At first it may feel strange or uncomfortable. But don't give up after the first or second time. And don't be discouraged by your mistakes. You need to make mistakes to learn. Mistakes show you where you need more practice. With practice, the new study skill will become more and more comfortable. And you'll begin to get good at it!

As you practice a new study skill, think a little bit about how you learn best: your *learning style*. Ask yourself: "What do I know about how I learn best that can help me learn this study skill?"

This Program can help you begin to learn 12 different study skills. You can learn any or all of them with a desire to learn and enough practice.

UNIT I
LEARNING TO LISTEN

QUESTIONS FOR GOOD LISTENERS

Directions: You are going to be involved in an activity to see how carefully you listen. Write your answers to each question that your teacher asks in the space provided.

1. _____
2. _____
3. _____
4. _____
5. _____
6. _____

LISTENING IS A SKILL

The average junior high or high school student spends about 55% of each day in school *listening*. That means that you give more time to listening than to anything else that you do in school.

Most people think of listening as something as natural as walking or eating. They don't think of it as anything you have to work at to do well. But as you've seen in the "Questions for Good Listeners," most of us are not naturally good listeners.

Why not? Hearing is a natural ability, but *listening* is more than just hearing. Listening means directing your attention to what you're hearing and trying to make sense of what you've heard.

Listening is a skill. It's one of the most important study skills because listening is a part of almost everything else that you do. It seems simple, but it's not. Being a good listener doesn't come naturally. It requires learning and practice.

WHY IS IT HARD TO LISTEN EVEN WHEN YOU'RE INTERESTED?

Generally people talk at about 125 words per minute. However, we think at a speed that is more than three times as fast, about 400 words per minute. That means that our thoughts move much faster than the words of whatever we're listening to. So, it's not surprising that we often let our attention wander away from what another person is saying to us.

The key to becoming a good listener is to be an *active* listener: to keep your thoughts directed on what you're listening to.

HOW CAN YOU BECOME AN ACTIVE LISTENER?

Being an active listener means both hearing the words that are being spoken and thinking about what those words mean. Below you'll find three helpful ways to think about what you're hearing:

1. While you listen, ask yourself questions about what the speaker is saying. Then, try to answer your questions. Asking and answering questions in this way can help you make sense of the speaker's message.

    ASK YOURSELF: What is the speaker telling me? Do I understand this? What don't I understand about what I'm hearing? Does this make sense to me?

2. Try to "picture" what you are hearing in your mind's eye. Some people can listen and understand better when they use their imaginations to make mental pictures of what they are hearing.

    ASK YOURSELF: Can I see a "picture" of what I'm hearing in my mind's eye?

3. Regularly summarize what the speaker has already said. Remind yourself of what's already been covered.

    ASK YOURSELF: What are the main points of what's already been said?

WHAT ELSE CAN YOU DO TO IMPROVE YOUR LISTENING SKILL?

1. Look at the person who is speaking. Establish eye contact if possible. This will help you to pay better attention to what he or she is saying.

2. *Listen first, judge later.* Listen to everything that the speaker has to say before you decide how you feel about it. If you begin to react in the middle of listening, then you may miss what he or she will say next. Try to listen to everything first. Then, react to it.

3. Take notes if you need to remember what's been said. (Units III and IV will help you with taking notes.)

EXERCISE I

Directions: Try to be an active listener while your teacher talks. Then, answer the questions below about what you have just heard.

1. What are the main points of what's been said?

   _____

   _____

   _____

   _____

2. Did you ask yourself any questions while you were listening? If you did, write one of the questions on the lines below.

   _____

   _____

   _____

3. Were you able to "picture" anything that you heard in your mind's eye? If you could, briefly describe one "picture" that you "saw" on the lines below.

   _____

   _____

   _____

   _____

4. Rate your *active listening* during the past few minutes on the scale below. Circle the number that you think best describes your listening.

not listening at all	listening at times	listening but not asking yourself any questions	listening and asking yourself some questions	active listening
1 2	3 4	5	6 7	8 9

LISTENING AND LEARNING STYLE

Some people seem to be able to learn by listening more easily than others. Learning by listening is a part of their learning style.

Do you know how well you learn by listening? Read the questions below, and think about your answers. Remember: there are no right or wrong answers!

1. Do you understand directions better when you can listen to them rather than read them?

2. Do you tend to remember what you hear on the radio?

3. Do you remember a story better when you can listen to it rather than see it acted out?

4. When you are learning something new, would you rather just start right in and try it or listen to someone explain it to you first?

UNIT I SUMMARY: LEARNING TO LISTEN

Listening is a skill. It takes effort and practice to learn how to be a good listener.

The key to being a good listener is to be an active listener. How do you become an active listener?

1. While you listen, ask yourself questions about what the speaker is saying. Then, try to answer your questions.

2. Try to "picture" what you are hearing in your mind's eye.

3. Regularly summarize what the speaker has already said.

4. Listen first, judge later. Don't try to evaluate what you are hearing until you've heard what the person has to say.

5. Take notes if you need to remember what's been said.

UNIT II
VOCABULARY: GETTING MEANING FROM CONTEXT

INTRODUCTION

Your vocabulary is your language. It's all the words that you understand and can use in your talking, writing, reading, and listening. If you only "sort of know" a word's meaning but can't use that word yourself, then it's not really a part of your vocabulary. Usually people need to see and use a word several times before they really know what it means.

This unit will show you a study skill that can help you increase your vocabulary and make your reading more interesting and enjoyable.

GETTING MEANING FROM CONTEXT CLUES

When you are reading, you often come across words that are unfamiliar or unknown to you. Two good ways that you can learn about the meaning of an unknown word are:

1. You can look it up in the dictionary.

    Looking it up immediately is particularly useful when you need to know an exact definition of the word.

2. Another way to learn about an unknown word is to try to figure out its meaning from context clues.

    CONTEXT means the setting in which something is found. For example a person lives in the context of his or her family. A clue in a mystery is only meaningful in the context of other information.

    In language, *context* means the words and sentences around any particular word.

    CONTEXT CLUES are familiar words and phrases in a sentence or paragraph. These are words that you know. From these familiar words, you can often figure out the meaning of an unknown word.

    Read the sentence below carefully. On the line beneath it, write down what you think the meaning of *curfew* is. Use context clues to help you discover that meaning.

    EXAMPLE: It's not unusual for young people to have a *curfew* set by their parents, for example, 11:30 PM or midnight.

curfew means _____

KINDS OF CONTEXT CLUES

There are four kinds of context clues with which you will work in this unit:

> definition or restatement
> example or description
> comparison or contrast
> inference

DEFINITION OR RESTATEMENT

Sometimes a sentence or paragraph actually includes a definition of the unknown word. It is usually not a dictionary definition, but it does tell you one meaning of the word.

Example of a Definition as a Context Clue

If your house *depreciates,* that means that it loses some of its value.

depreciate means _____

At times authors will use a difficult or uncommon word and feel a need to explain its meaning. One way in which they do this is *restatement:* to include the meaning of the difficult word in the same sentence in which they use that word. Another way in which they do this is to include a synonym for the difficult word in the same sentence.

Example of a Restatement as a Context Clue

One of the weapons available to a government is *propaganda,* the spreading of its own narrow and often false views.

propaganda _____

EXERCISE 1

Directions: Circle the words in each sentence below that are context clues to the meaning of the italicized word.

1. A *facsimile* is always an exact copy.

2. They had already begun to *dismantle* the ship, taking it apart piece by piece.

3. The workers built a *trestle,* a braced framework made of wood, as a support for the railroad tracks where they crossed a stream.

4. An *hypothesis* is a proposed explanation for an event or a group of events. It is often used to guide investigation in scientific study.

EXAMPLE OR DESCRIPTION

In its context, an unknown word may be followed by examples that can give you an idea of what the word means. The examples may also come before the unknown word. With this kind of context clue, you can gain a sense of what the unfamiliar word means by looking at the examples.

Example of Examples as Context Clues

The *sweatshops* where many poor immigrants worked were characterized by overcrowding, poor heat and ventilation, no fire escapes, and very low wages.

sweatshop means _____

Another kind of context clue like examples is a description, a clause or phrase that tells you about the meaning of an unknown word. A description gives you a word picture of something or shows you some of its parts. The description usually comes after the unknown word.

Example of a Description as a Context Clue

When I *procrastinate* and put off working on a project day after day until just before it is due, I usually don't do as good a job as I am capable of doing.

procrastinate means _____

EXERCISE II

Directions: Write a definition for each italicized word below on the lines provided. Use context clues to develop your definition.

1. Should our society have a *censor* who would decide what books and movies should not be available to children?

   censor means _____

2. Animals are divided into invertebrates and *vertebrates*. Monkeys belong to the *vertebrates* because they have backbones.

   vertebrate means _____

3. Squares, rectangles, and trapezoids are all *quadrilaterals*.

   quadrilateral means _____

4. Some dishonest wine makers have been known to *adulterate* their expensive wines by adding water or cheaper wine to them.

   adulterate means _____

COMPARISON OR CONTRAST

One kind of context clue is given when the author tells you about an unknown word by *comparing* it with something else. A comparison tells you what something is like. By knowing what something is similar to, you can often gain a sense of what it is.

Example of a Comparison as a Context Clue

Her *predicament* presented her with the same difficult problem she had faced the year before when her family had moved for the first time.

predicament means _____

Another kind of context clue is given when the author tells you about an unknown word by *contrasting* it with something else. A contrast tells you what something is not like. By knowing what something is different from, you can often get an idea of what it is.

Example of a Contrast as a Context Clue

Instead of being *demoted* as she had feared, she was offered a new and more challenging job that paid more.

demoted means _____

EXERCISE III

Directions: Write a definition for each italicized word below on the lines provided. Use context clues to develop your definitions.

1. Rather than the usual 20 devoted fans, the basketball team found a large *throng* awaiting their return at the airport.

   throng means _____

2. Her *prowess* on the parallel bars is like the skillful daring of a great acrobat.

   prowess means _____

3. This year's yard sale was a *fiasco*. They earned even less money than they did last year.

   fiasco means _____

4. At first people thought that television would make radio *obsolete,* but it's turned out that millions of people still listen to radio.

   obsolete means _____

INFERENCE

An *inference* is a conclusion or idea that you create by examining various facts and then making a reasonable judgment based on those facts. For example, you can often *infer* what the menu will be at lunch by walking past the cafeteria and recognizing the smells of the various foods.

Sometimes you can infer the meaning of an unknown word by examining the meanings of the words and phrases around it. Even when there are none of the special kinds of context clues about which you have learned in this unit, the context of the unknown word can sometimes still help you understand the meaning of that word.

Example of an Inference as a Context Clue

If you've ever gone on a blind date, you've probably experienced that moment of *trepidation* just before you meet your date for the first time.

trepidation means _____

EXERCISE IV

Directions: Write a definition for each italicized word below on the lines provided. Use context clues to develop your definitions.

1. I'm a very friendly person. I always like to be with people, either doing things that we enjoy or just talking. I suppose that's why people say I'm *gregarious*.

    gregarious means _____

2. There are still no cures for the common cold. The medicines that people take for a cold are simply *palliatives* which help them to feel a little better for a few hours at a time.

    palliative means _____

3. The *tortuous* road we had to climb had one steep and narrow curve after another all the way to the top. That's probably why it's called Snake Hill Road.

    tortuous means _____

4. I like Mary because she's not *exclusive*. When she has a party, she invites the whole class, not just her best friends.

    exclusive means _____

HINTS FOR USING CONTEXT CLUES

1. When you come to an unknown word as you read, stopping to look it up in the dictionary can interfere with the flow of your reading. Instead of looking it up, try to use context clues to get a sense of the unknown word's meaning. Then, you can keep on with your reading.

2. When you can figure out the meaning of an unknown word from context clues, quickly jot that word down. Then, when you come to a natural break in your reading, look the word up in the dictionary. Check to see how close your context definition is to the dictionary definition.

3. When you can't figure out the meaning of an unknown word from context clues, you need to look up the word when you want to learn what it means.

EXERCISE V

Directions: Write a definition for each italicized word below on the lines provided. Use context clues to develop your definitions.

1. They were lying on their stomachs, *inert,* like dead men except for the soft hum of their breathing.

   inert means _____

2. They had to bring in *mercenaries* or hired soldiers to fight the war.

   mercenaries means _____

3. The *surveillance* of the suspect's house went on for more than a week, but the police learned nothing new from all their hours of waiting and watching.

   surveillance means _____

4. After working for two years in the dark, overheated office, Felicia developed such a *loathing* for the place that she vowed to find another job as soon as she possibly could.

   loathing means _____

5. The talk show host always *gesticulated* as he spoke, moving his arms and hands to help him welcome guests, praise them, ask them questions, and even make fun of them.

   gesticulated means _____

Continued on the next page.

6. Our lungs and other parts of the *respiratory* system enable us to breathe.

   respiratory means _____

7. The mayor's waiting room used to be full of *petitioners* who were seeking special favors.

   petitioner means _____

8. Rather than *disparage* people when they make mistakes, you should try to praise them when they do things correctly.

   disparage means _____

9. Claude has become such a good mechanic that I can't *differentiate* between his work and work done by the man who owns the garage.

   differentiate means _____

10. The brothers were very different. One was *parsimonious* while the other spent his money like water.

    parsimonious means _____

11. Many animals such as dinosaurs are now *extinct*.

    extinct means _____

12. The disease brought with it a feeling of *lassitude* which made her feel like lying in bed all day.

    lassitude means _____

13. To *emote* or express one's feelings is usually very healthy.

    emote means _____

14. At election time people face a difficult *dilemma* if they don't like any of the candidates who are on the ballot.

    dilemma means _____

15. Jack told his friends that he had already ignored several *provocations,* such as curses directed at him and a snowball thrown at his head.

    provocation means _____

EXERCISE VI

Directions: Write a definition for each italicized word below on the lines provided. Use context clues to develop your definitions.

1. The President has a group of people who travel with him wherever he goes. Some of them are bodyguards. Others are aides and advisors. Even when he's with his family, this *entourage* is never far away.

   entourage means _____

2. Even as a child Denise liked to watch birds in flight and paint pictures of them. "When I grow up," she told herself, "I'll spend all of my time learning about birds." Now, after all these years of preparation, she is finally an *ornithologist*.

   ornithologist means _____

3. Wood is *opaque*. So are concrete and iron. But glass and water are not *opaque*.

   opaque means _____

4. It takes a lot of *stamina* for a runner to complete a marathon. She or he must have both strength and endurance.

   stamina means _____

5. He had known her for little more than a week. He'd only talked with her twice, but he'd already sent her flowers three times. Clearly, he was *infatuated* with her.

   infatuated means _____

6. The lifeguard worked on the man for almost five minutes before he was able to *resuscitate* him.

   resuscitate means _____

7. She explained that she had only two *siblings,* a brother and a sister.

   sibling means _____

8. In April Roberto spent a week hiking through the mountains alone. Many of his friends thought he was foolish for undertaking such a project. Yet when he returned, they were all eager to know how his *solitary* week had gone.

   solitary means _____

Continued on the next page.

9. Before people learned that the Earth was round, they did not know that they could *circumnavigate* the globe in ships.

   circumnavigate means _____

10. Sheila and her friends had gone to the museum without bothering to check the price of admission. They had expected to pay two dollars or more to get in and were happy to learn that there was only a *nominal* charge for students.

    nominal means _____

11. He suffered from *amnesia* and could remember neither his name nor his address.

    amnesia means _____

12. This document contains every word that was said in the courtroom. If you read this *verbatim* account of the trial, you will know what went on.

    verbatim means _____

13. The officer thought that Robert was *inebriated* because his car was weaving across the road. It took Robert a long time to convince the officer that he had not been drinking and that the car was weaving because his steering had failed.

    inebriated means _____

14. The students at this school are a *heterogeneous* group. They include people of every race and major religious group in the world.

    heterogeneous means _____

15. She put on her protective gear and headed out to the *apiary* to collect a fresh supply of honey.

    apiary means _____

A FINAL HINT ABOUT CONTEXT CLUES

Context clues can often help you figure out the meanings of unknown or unfamiliar words in your reading. But you can't rely only on context clues to learn new words. You need to use a dictionary as well.

How do you know when to stop your reading and use a dictionary? When you are using context clues to understand unfamiliar or unknown words but the reading makes less and less sense to you as you go along, it is probably time to use a dictionary to look up the meanings of the unknown words.

UNIT II SUMMARY: VOCABULARY: GETTING MEANING FROM CONTEXT

One good way to figure out the meaning of an unknown word is to use *context clues*.

The *context* is the setting in which the unknown word is found — the words, phrases, and sentences around it. *Context clues* are familiar words and phrases. From the meaning of these, you can often figure out the meaning of the unknown word.

The kinds of *context clues* are:

1. Definition or restatement

    The context actually includes a definition of the unknown word. Or, the context gives you a restatement of it, expressing its meaning in other words.

2. Example or description

    The context includes examples of the unknown word that can give you an idea of its meaning. Or, the context describes the meaning of the unknown word.

3. Comparison or contrast

    The context tells you what the unknown word is like or what it's not like.

4. Inference

    The context gives you enough information about the unknown word so that you can draw some reasonable conclusions about, or infer, its meaning.

When you read, try to use *context clues* to gain a sense of the meaning of an unknown or unfamiliar word. Then, look up the unknown word in the dictionary when you come to a natural break in your reading. See how close your context definition is to the dictionary definition.

UNIT III
NOTE TAKING METHODS

WHY TAKE NOTES?

The major difficulty that many students have in taking notes is that they're not really sure what they're trying to accomplish. Some students try to copy down every word. Others may only write down a few facts here and there without including any ideas that explain them.

The purpose of taking notes is to help you learn.

To take useful notes, you need to figure out what's important in what you are reading or hearing. You want to write down only the main ideas and important details. Figuring out what you want to include in your notes and jotting it down will help you learn these ideas and details.

Taking notes also gives you a record of what you need to know for the future. Then, you can use your notes to study for tests.

Think of your notes as a road map. What you want to write down as notes are words and phrases that will help you to remember the main ideas and important details of what you've read or heard. Just as a road map leaves out a lot of detail, so can your notes.

Always write your notes in your own words. When you put notes into your own words, you can be sure that you understand what your notes mean. You'll also understand them when you come back to them later.

So, taking notes helps you to learn when you first write them down. It also gives you a record that you can use later.

NOTE TAKING METHODS

This unit will show you two effective ways of taking notes: *outlining* and *mapping*. Try both of these methods, and see how each one works for you.

This unit will also show you a method you can use to save time when you're taking notes.

OUTLINING

An outline is a way of organizing and listing ideas and information from a written or spoken presentation. To create an outline, first decide what the main idea of the presentation is. Then, below the main idea, list the important details that relate to the main idea.

Read the paragraph below. Following it, you will find an outline that is a good example of notes for that paragraph.

Paragraph I

As a result of the 18th Amendment to the Constitution, Prohibition went into effect in all parts of the United States on January 20, 1920. This amendment made the manufacture and use of alcohol illegal, unless it was for medical, industrial, or religious purposes. The Volstead Act was passed by Congress to make it possible for the government to enforce Prohibition. It set up an agency of 1,500 agents who tried to make sure that the law was obeyed. However, during the next 13 years, the law did not stop many people from drinking alcoholic beverages. Instead, it led to the creation of a large business for criminals who illegally made liquor and sold it in bars called "speakeasies" or by the bottle. Some people made their own liquor, often called "moonshine" or "bathtub gin," at home. The 18th Amendment was finally repealed in 1933. The era of Prohibition was over.

Outline for Paragraph I

I. Prohibition — illegal to make, use alcohol
   A. 18th amendment — began 1920
   B. Volstead Act — agents to enforce it
   C. Didn't work — criminals ignored it, so did many others
   D. Ended 1933

HOW TO OUTLINE

1. First, read the whole paragraph or section for which you're taking notes.

2. Decide what the main idea is. Write down the main idea in your own words. Use Roman numerals to indicate main ideas. Look at the "outline form" below to see how this is done.

3. Then, decide which details are important. Ask yourself: which details support the main idea? List these supporting details below the main idea. Use capital letters to indicate supporting details.

4. When you need to list information under the items indicated by capital letters, use numbers. Look at the "outline form" to see how this is done.

OUTLINE FORM

I. Main idea
   A. Supporting detail
   B. Supporting detail
      1. Sub-detail
      2. Sub-detail

TIPS FOR TAKING NOTES

1. Always write your notes in your own words (unless you are copying a quotation). Putting ideas and information into your own words helps you to understand them and learn them better.

2. Just try to get the main ideas and important, supporting details down on paper!

3. Try to spend 80-90% of your time reading or listening, and only 10-20% of your time writing notes.

4. Write your notes in words and phrases. Don't bother to use complete sentences. Your notes are for you! Write them in the quickest way that makes sense to you.

EXERCISE I

Directions: Read the following paragraph, and take notes for it in the outline form below.

During the 19th century, women in America had very few rights. All children were considered to be the property of their fathers. When a woman married, she once again belonged to a man, this time her husband. The husband became the legal owner of all of her property and earnings. Also, women were not allowed to vote or hold public office. Generally, women were considered inferior to men and, thus, not deserving of rights. It was not until the 20th century that women began to win these rights in most states.

I. _____

   A. _____

   B. _____

   C. _____

   D. _____

MAPPING

Another good way of organizing ideas and information on paper is mapping. Instead of using numbers and letters to organize your notes, you make a diagram or map with your notes.

Read the paragraph below. Under it, you'll find a map that is a good example of notes for that paragraph.

Paragraph II

Wildlife refuges are areas where wild animals and the environment in which they live are protected from people. Either no hunting at all is allowed, or the amount of hunting is carefully controlled. Most wildlife refuges are owned by the local, state, or federal governments. People are not allowed to live in these areas or use the land for any purpose that would be harmful to the animals. Efforts are made to preserve the land as it is naturally. Also, winter feeding for the animals is provided in many refuges.

Map For Paragraph II

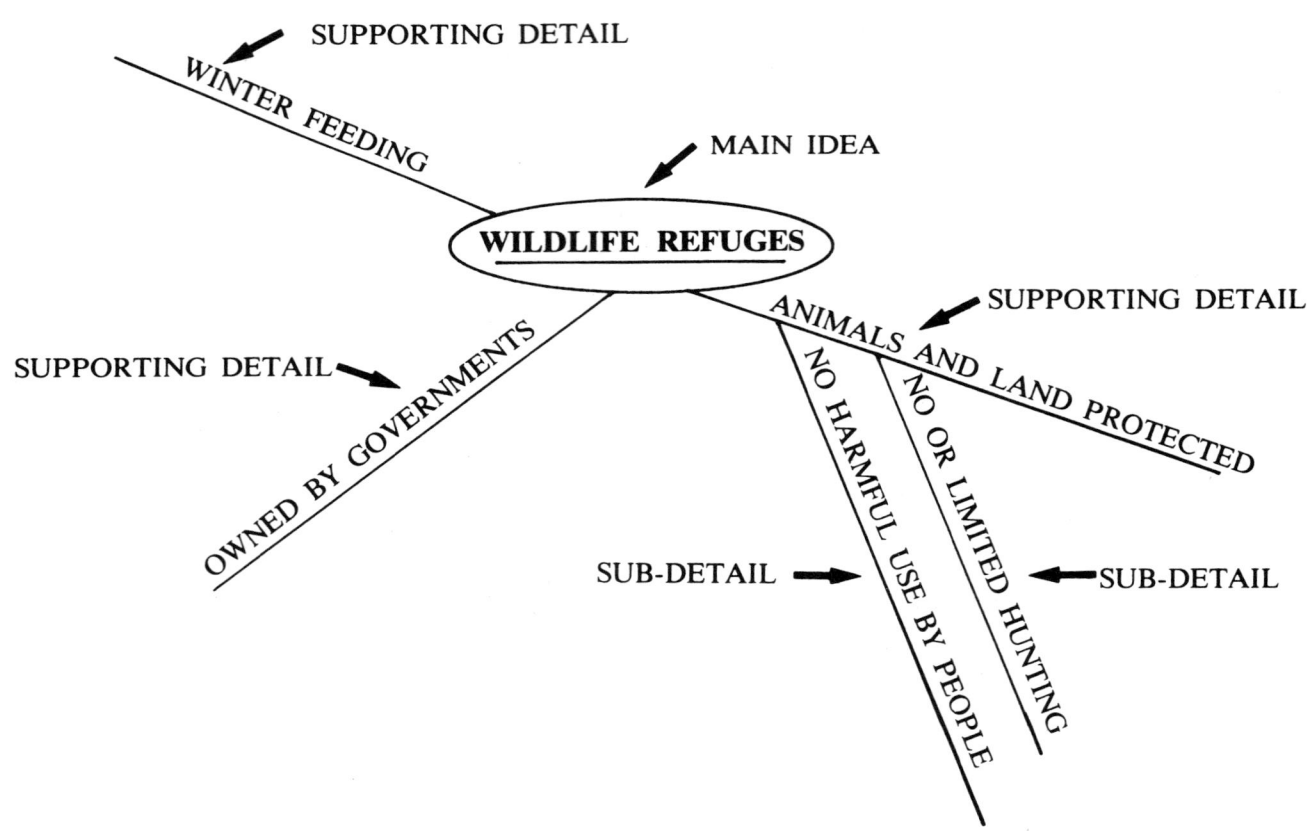

HOW TO MAP

1. First, read the whole paragraph or section for which you are taking notes.

2. Decide what the main idea is. Then, print or write the main idea in the center of your page. Circle it.

3. Print or write the important, supporting details on lines that are connected to the circle around the main idea. Look at the map on page 22 to see how this is done.

4. When you need to include more information under the supporting details, print or write these sub-details on lines that are connected to the lines of the supporting details. Look at the map on page 22 to see how this is done.

REMEMBER: When you are mapping, be sure to connect all notes to some other note in a way that makes sense to you. Then, when you finish, your notes will already be organized.

EXERCISE II

Directions: Read the paragraph below, and take notes for it using the mapping form that follows it.

The air over most cities is polluted. It contains substances released from cars and trucks, industrial smokestacks, and houses and other buildings. As it contains some poisonous materials, polluted air is harmful to health as well as unpleasant to breathe. It can make people cough, choke, cry, and even faint. More seriously, it can also cause respiratory infections, lung cancer, allergies, and several other diseases. Polluted air also hurts plants and reduces the yield of agricultural crops.

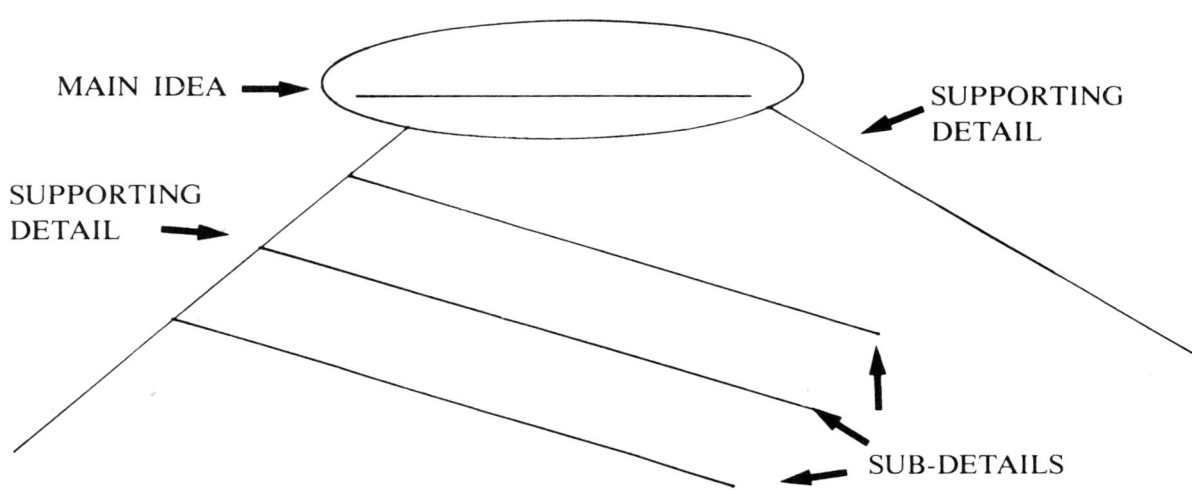

EXERCISE III

Directions: In Exercise II, you took mapping notes for a paragraph in which the supporting details were not in a sequence. You did not need to write them in order. The paragraph below has a different kind of organization. You can note its supporting details most clearly by putting them into a sequence.

Read the paragraphs below. Then, map these paragraphs on page 25. Invent a way to show the supporting details so that their sequence is clear.

Hint: There are many ways in which you can show a sequence in a map! There is no one right way.

Iron is the most used metal. Nearly 600 million tons of iron are produced throughout the world every year. It is the least costly and most versatile metallic building material. There are few places where metals other than iron must be used.

The purest form of iron in common use is wrought iron. This iron is made by the refining of iron ore. Wrought iron contains carbon and small amounts of other elements as impurities. Its properties are such that its range of use is very limited. Most iron is changed into steel in a second refining step in which *some* of the carbon is removed. Steel is an *alloy* — a mixture of iron with other elements.

The properties of iron and its alloy, steel, change greatly with carbon content. Pure iron, which has been made for laboratory use, is silvery white, fairly soft, and magnetic. Wrought iron, containing a little carbon, is much harder, but it can still be worked and hammered easily. Steel varies in its properties from "soft steel" with little carbon content, to tougher and stronger steel with greater amounts of carbon.

Aluminum is the metal next in importance to iron. Almost 11 million tons of aluminum are produced throughout the world each year. An important and useful property of aluminum is its low density, about one-third that of iron. In addition, aluminum is a good conductor of electricity, making it suitable for electricity transmission lines.

Copper is the third most important metal, in terms of tons produced. World production totals about 7.1 million tons a year. Small amounts of copper are used to make alloys like brass and bronze. Most of the copper produced is used in electrical equipment because it is the best conductor among the common metals.

Only two other metals are used in any significant amounts. The yearly world production of zinc is just over 5.5 million tons. Zinc is used mainly in the protection of steel against rusting. Yearly world production of lead is almost 4 million tons.

Notes for Exercise III

USING ABBREVIATIONS AND SYMBOLS IN NOTE TAKING

One good way to save time when you're taking notes is to use abbreviations and symbols whenever you can. You can use abbreviations and symbols that are generally accepted, and you can develop your own as well.

An abbreviation is several letters taken from a word that are used to stand for that word.

Examples of abbreviations:

word	abbreviation
continued	cont.
United States of America	USA
mathematics	math
government	govt.

A symbol is a letter or marking that is used to stand for a word or words.

Examples of symbols:

word	symbol
with	w
and	+
without	w/o

EXERCISE IV

Directions: Create a symbol or abbreviation for each of the following words.

1. California _____

2. equals _____

3. department _____

4. against _____

5. leads to _____

6. because _____

7. biology _____

8. information _____

9. decrease _____

TAKING USEFUL NOTES

Many people prefer to take notes in outline form. Others prefer mapping. Some people use methods other than these two to take notes. Do you know other ways of taking notes?

Some people learn more than one method for taking notes, for example, outlining and mapping. Then, they can use outlining in some situations and mapping in others.

What is most important is that you learn a way of taking notes that makes sense to you. Practice both mapping and outlining for awhile. Then, use the method of note taking which works best for you as a learner. Or, become skillful at using both of these methods, and use them in different situations.

UNIT III SUMMARY: NOTE TAKING METHODS

Taking notes helps you to learn in two ways:

1. To take good notes, you need to figure out what the important ideas and details are in what you're reading or hearing. Figuring out what these important ideas and details are and then writing them down will help you to learn them.

2. You can use your notes a week or a month later to study for a test.

Think of your notes as a MAP. Write down only the main ideas and important details. Also, be sure to write your notes in your own words.

Two good methods for taking notes are:

1. OUTLINING

    I. Main idea
       A. Supporting detail
       B. Supporting detail
          1. Sub-detail
          2. Sub-detail

2. MAPPING

```
SUPPORTING DETAIL          SUPPORTING DETAIL
              ( MAIN IDEA )
SUPPORTING DETAIL        SUB-DETAIL  SUB-DETAIL
```

Use abbreviations and symbols as much as possible when you take notes. The more you can use them, the less writing you'll have to do, and the more time you will have for reading and listening.

UNIT IV
LISTENING AND TAKING NOTES

INTRODUCTION

In the previous unit, you learned about two ways of taking notes: outlining and mapping. You practiced both of these methods to take notes from reading.

In this unit, you'll learn how you can use these methods to take notes from listening.

WHY TAKE NOTES IN CLASS?

Much of what you need to learn to do well in any subject will be covered in class. However, just hearing something once in class doesn't mean you will learn it. Most people need to hear something several times or to write it down before they can really learn it.

One way to learn in class is to take brief notes about what you've heard. Taking brief notes will help you learn in three ways:

1. Taking notes will help you focus on the main ideas and important details of what's being said, because you'll only want to write down the main ideas and important details.

2. Writing down the main ideas and important details as notes will help you to learn them.

3. You can use the notes that you've taken later on when you want to study for a test.

REMEMBER: Taking notes helps you to learn both when you first write the notes down and when you use them for studying.

HOW DO YOU START?

Before you begin to take notes in class, you need to decide which method to use. For most people, the following suggestions will be helpful:

1. You can use the outline method for a lecture or any kind of organized talk. Sometimes your teacher may put an outline on the board either before he or she begins to talk or as he or she goes along. Use this outline as a starting point for your outline. Even if an outline is not given, you can still take outline notes for any organized talk.

2. You can use the mapping method for taking notes during any activity that is less organized, such as a class discussion or question period. When you use mapping, you can organize the ideas on your paper as you go along.

3. If you feel very comfortable with any one method of taking notes, then use it whenever you can! Some people find that one way of taking notes fits in with their learning style, and they can do their best work using only that one method.

It may seem difficult at first to know which method to use for taking notes. Don't worry about this! With a little practice, you'll discover how you can best take notes that make sense to you.

WHAT TO KEEP IN MIND ABOUT LISTENING AND TAKING NOTES

1. Be an active listener! Ask yourself questions about what the speaker is saying. Then, try to answer the questions. Try to "picture" what you are hearing in your mind's eye. Regularly summarize what the speaker has already said. Listen first, judge later!

2. Try to spend most of your time listening. As you listen, figure out what the main ideas and important details are. Then, write them down. Use your own words. Remember: your notes are for you.

3. When your teacher tells you that you'll need to know something, be sure to write it down in your notes.

EXERCISE I

Directions: Your teacher will deliver a short lecture. Take outline notes from it on the lines below. Use the brief outline that he or she puts on the board as a starting point for your notes.

EXERCISE II

Directions: Your teacher will lead a short class discussion. Take mapping notes for this discussion in the space below.

UNIT IV SUMMARY: LISTENING AND TAKING NOTES

Taking brief notes in class can help you to learn both when you first write the notes down and when you use them for studying.

1. You can use the outline method to take notes for a lecture or any kind of organized presentation.

2. You can use the mapping method to take notes for any class activity that is less organized, such as a class discussion.

3. If you feel particularly comfortable with any one way of taking notes, use the method whenever you can.

Remember to be an active listener!

UNIT V
A WAY TO READ TEXTBOOKS

INTRODUCTION

A large part of the school work that any high school student does is reading. You read short stories, novels, newspaper and magazine articles, poems, plays, and so on, but much of the reading you do is in textbooks.

EXERCISE I

Directions: Think about the ways that textbooks are different from novels and stories. List three of these differences on the lines below.

1. _____

2. _____

3. _____

HOW DO YOU READ A TEXTBOOK?

Many students read a textbook exactly the same way they read a short story or a novel. They start with the first word on the first page and read straight through until they come to the last word of the assignment.

However, as you've seen above, a textbook is very different from a short story or a novel. People write textbooks to help the reader learn the information inside them as easily as possible. Most textbooks are divided into chapters. The chapters, in turn, are divided into sections, which usually have headings above them.

Think of the chapter titles and section headings as *road signs*. They tell you where the textbook is going, what the next chapter or section is about.

It makes sense, then, to read a textbook in a special way, one that takes advantage of these signs.

A WAY TO READ TEXTBOOKS

The way of reading textbooks that this unit will show you has three steps:

>survey
>read and take notes
>review

1. ## SURVEY

   Before you start to read the textbook, take 2-3 minutes to survey your assignment. This means to read the chapter title, introduction, and section headings. Also, be sure to read the summary or conclusion and any review questions at the end of the chapter.

   As you survey, ask yourself: "What is this reading about? What are the main ideas here? What do I already know about this? What do I need to learn?" Ask yourself questions like these, and then answer them.

2. ## READ AND TAKE NOTES

   Once you have surveyed a section or chapter in your textbook, the next step is to read it carefully.

   Also, decide if you want to take notes for this reading. As you have already discovered, taking notes both helps you learn as you read and gives you a record of the reading that you can use later on. When you will need to know about this reading later on, then you'll probably want to take notes.

   If you are going to take notes, decide which note taking method you will use. Always read a whole section before you start to take your notes.

3. ## REVIEW

   When you have finished reading your assignment, then it's time to review. Review means to take a few minutes and go over the main ideas and important details that you have just read. You can do this in your head, by talking with a friend, and/or by going over your notes.

   When you review ask yourself: "What's important for me to learn from this reading? What are the main ideas? Is there anything here that I don't understand? If so, how will I find out about it?" Ask yourself questions like these, and then answer them.

   When you take notes from your readings, you can use your notes as part of your review. Read through your notes to go over the main ideas and make sure that these make sense to you.

   Many textbooks include "questions for study" at the end of each chapter. You can also use these questions to help you review. Ask yourself each "question for study," and then answer it. If you can't answer any of the questions, go back to the reading to find the answer.

   The purpose of reviewing is to help you *really learn* the main ideas and important details that you have just read. When you take a few minutes to review, you'll be able to remember much more about what you have read.

EXERCISE II

Directions: Read the textbook section below using the three step method described on page 34. If you are uncertain about any of the steps, look back at the explanations on page 34.

Take notes for this reading in the space provided on page 36. Use a note taking method of your choice.

TEXTBOOK SECTION I

A NEW WAY TO TRAVEL. Automobiles are so important today that it is hard to think of a time when we did not have them. Yet you can find people today who can remember when a car was something new.

The internal-combustion engine burns a fuel inside itself and uses the heat to provide power. It was developed in Europe. It opened the way for men to invent the automobile and later the airplane. One of the German-made "horseless carriages" was brought to our country. It was studied by Charles E. and J. Frank Duryea. In 1893 they drove down the streets of their city in a gasoline-powered car they had designed and built.

The next year, in 1894, the Apperson brothers and Jonathan Maxwell built a car planned by Elwood G. Haynes. These men helped start our auto industry. Within a few years other men, inventors and mechanics, were turning out automobiles of their own. This new business used the skills we had developed in the carriage business. Men like the Studebakers of South Bend, Indiana, found it easy to shift from one business to the other.

Some of our first automobiles were powered by steam or electricity. Cars that used gasoline were much better; before long, we gave up the other types.

What did these early cars look like? They were not at all like the ones you see today. They weren't big, shiny, or powerful. Their tires were poorly made. These cars broke down easily on hard drives. You had to be a mechanic to keep one running well. But when they ran, they got you there. People bought them. This was a way to travel!

CHANGES BROUGHT BY THE AUTOMOBILE. In less than twenty-five years we had given up the use of horses for travel and moving goods. Today, much of our country's wealth depends upon the automobile. It is one of our largest industries. Many other businesses supply the automobile makers. Automobiles need rubber; they need electric equipment; they need cloth and glass and plastic; they need paint and special metals. As we began to use more automobiles, our country built better surfaced roads; today we have the best roads in the world.

The automobile has brought us many problems, too. Every year thousands of people are killed or hurt in accidents. More of our people have been killed in cars than in all the wars our country has fought. How can we end this waste of life? We still seek an answer to this great national problem.

Notes for Exercise II

WHAT ARE THE ADVANTAGES OF THE SURVEY, READ AND TAKE NOTES, REVIEW METHOD?

1. Using this method can help you become an active reader, one who reads to understand and learn rather than just turning the pages and getting it over with. If you are an active reader, you'll find that your reading will be more interesting to you.

2. Using the survey, read and take notes, review method will help you to learn more when you read and remember more about what you've read. This method is designed to make the most of the way your memory works.

3. When you decide to take notes from your reading as a part of this method, you'll remember more about what you've read. Also, you'll have a record of the reading with which you can study.

4. Although it will probably take you a little more time to use the survey, read and take notes, review method at first, once you learn how to do it you'll find that it can be as fast as your old method ... and much more effective! Practice this method three or four times, and you'll soon see how quickly you can become comfortable with it.

TIPS FOR TAKING NOTES FROM YOUR READING

1. Always use your own words in your notes. Putting ideas and information into your own words is a good way to learn about them.

2. Write your notes in words and phrases, not in complete sentences. Use abbreviations and symbols to save time.

3. Remember that your notes are for you, not for anyone else. Take notes that make sense to you.

EXERCISE III

Directions: Use the survey, read and take notes, review method to read the textbook sections below. Write your notes for these sections in the space provided on page 39.

TEXTBOOK SECTION II

A FLYING MACHINE. Men long dreamed of being able to fly. However, they had never had a way to keep a heavier-than-air "ship" up in the air. Then, in 1903, two young bicycle mechanics, Wilbur and Orville Wright, placed a motor on their flying machine. It turned a propeller which made the air flow in a way that kept their machine up in the air. Their first flight was at Kitty Hawk, North Carolina. They kept their plane in the air for several hundred feet. They had invented the first true airplane.

They were not the first to try. Back in the 1700's balloons had been invented which were large enough to carry a basket with people in it. Many hoped this would be the beginning of flying. But these balloons were dangerous; it was hard to control their flight.

The next step came after 1800. Men in both Europe and America worked with gliders. These were built of light wood, and used wind currents to keep them up in the air. The Wright brothers had worked with gliders, too. They learned much about what was needed to make an airplane fly. They had to control the wind currents to keep their plane up. They built a box-like plane and a gasoline engine to power it. Then, even though the world took little notice at first, they made their machine fly.

AVIATION IMPROVES. Aviation is the science of building and flying airplanes. We have learned much about aviation since the days of the Wright brothers. They and other men in many parts of the world worked for the next ten years to make better planes. Then, in 1914, a world war began. Both sides built planes and trained young pilots. The airplanes they flew in that war were slow, and did not fly well. Stories are told of pilots in the First World War who flew wing tip to wing tip and fought it out with blazing revolvers!

Aviation boomed after the war. Men set up companies to build and sell airplanes. Daring pilots made long trips. Some died; others became famous. In 1927 young Charles A. Lindbergh surprised the world by flying his plane, the "Spirit of St. Louis," from New York to Paris, France. He flew alone for 3,610 miles across the Atlantic. His success showed our people that air travel had a great future. More people were willing to invest their money in the new industry.

Notes for Exercise III

UNIT V SUMMARY: A WAY TO READ TEXTBOOKS

Textbooks are very different from novels, short stories, and plays. Textbooks are written in a special way to help the reader learn the information within them as easily as possible. They are usually organized into chapters and sections, with chapter titles and section headlines.

A way of reading textbooks that takes advantage of this organization is the survey, read and take notes, review method.

SURVEY   Quickly look over the chapter title, introduction, section headings, and conclusion or summary to get an idea of what the chapter is about. Also, read any questions for study that you find at the end of the chapter.

READ AND TAKE NOTES   Read the chapter carefully. Take notes if you will need to recall the information in the chapter later on.

REVIEW   Go over the main ideas and important details in the chapter. Ask yourself: "What do I need to learn from this reading?" Then, answer your question.

UNIT VI
SOLVING PROBLEMS

A "PARTY PROBLEM"

Imagine that you are facing the problem described in the paragraph below.

You are going to have a party at your house on Friday night. Among the people you want to invite are two friends — let's call them person A and person B — who don't like each other very much. In fact, once before when you invited both of them to do something with you, they both said afterwards that they would prefer not to see each other in the future. Yet you want to invite both of them to the party, both because you'd enjoy having them there and because you don't want to offend either of them by only inviting the other.

What would you do to solve this problem? On the lines below, list at least one *strategy* that you could use to solve this problem. A *strategy* is a way or method or process for solving a problem. It's not the solution or answer itself but, rather, how you can find the solution or answer.

Don't actually solve the problem now. You'll get a chance to do that in a few minutes. Just describe one *strategy* you could use to find a solution to the "party problem."

_____

_____

_____

_____

_____

_____

WHAT IS A PROBLEM?

A problem is any situation in which you have a starting point, a set of directions, and the need to create an answer or solution. There are many different kinds of problems. For example, the "party" problem on the previous page, the word problems in your math book, the lab problems in your science class, and the problem of finding time for all you want to do are very different from each other. Yet they are all problems.

This unit will introduce you to a five step method for solving problems. It is a method that you can apply to almost any kind of problem that you need to solve.

The steps in this method are:

1. Defining the problem.
2. Listing possible strategies for solving the problem.
3. Examining your list of strategies, and choosing the best one.
4. Trying out your best strategy.
5. Trying another strategy if your first choice doesn't work.

EXERCISE I

Directions: Work through the steps of the five step problem solving method as the directions indicate below. Apply each step to the "party problem."

STEP ONE

Tell yourself exactly what the problem is. Also, include any information you know about what kind of solution you are seeking.

Directions: Write your description of the "party problem" on the lines below.

_____
_____
_____
_____
_____
_____

STEP TWO

Think of at least 2-3 strategies that you might use to solve the problem. Make a list of these strategies.

You've already done this step. Use the list of strategies that your teacher has written on the board.

STEP THREE

Examine your list of possible strategies, and choose the one that seems best.

Directions: Go over the list of strategies that your teacher has written on the board. Write the one that seems best on the lines below.

_____

_____

_____

STEP FOUR

Try out your best strategy, and see if it works to solve the problem.

Directions: You can't actually do this now, but you can imagine how you think it would work. On the lines below, briefly describe how you think the strategy you chose would work to solve the "party problem." To what solution do you think it would bring you? How would you feel about this solution?

_____

_____

_____

_____

_____

_____

_____

STEP FIVE

If your best strategy doesn't work, go back to your list of possible strategies in Step Two, and pick another one to try.

Or, you can try the following:

A. Stop thinking about the problem, and come back to it in a day or two.

    Sometimes when you try to solve a problem and you're stuck, the best thing you can do is to go away from the problem for awhile. Often your mind will go right on "thinking" about the problem without your being aware of it. Sometimes a good strategy will just pop up in front of you. Other times the solution itself may appear. This is what happens, for example, when you are trying to remember a name — it's right on the tip of your tongue — but you can't quite get it. When you stop trying to remember it, the name will often just pop into your mind a few minutes later.

B. Research the problem, and then start again with Step Two.

    Sometimes when you can't solve a problem, it's because you don't know enough about it. To research a problem means to learn more about it. Ask people about it who might know more than you do. Find ways to read about it if you can. Then, when you know more, go through the steps of this method again.

EXERCISE II

Directions: Solve problems #1, #2, and #3 using the five steps described above. For all three problems, describe the strategy you use as well as writing the solution in the appropriate space.

1. Below you will find three different views of the same block. The six faces of the block are marked with different letters.

    — Which letter is opposite the b?
    — Which letter is opposite the e?
    — Which letter is opposite the a?

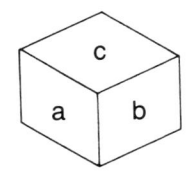

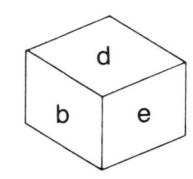

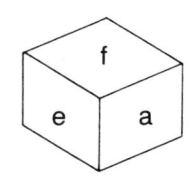

    On the lines below, describe the strategy that you will use to solve this problem.

    _____

    _____

    _____

    Which letter is opposite the b? _____

    Which letter is opposite the e? _____

    Which letter is opposite the a? _____

2. A truck driver leaves Dubuque at 10:00 AM and starts driving west. At 10:40 AM the truck crosses a bridge 51 miles west of Dubuque. Why does the state police officer pull up next to the truck and signal the driver to stop?

On the lines below, describe the strategy you will use to solve this problem.

___

Why does the state police officer pull up next to the truck and signal the driver to stop?

___

3. You want to go out with your friends on Saturday night to see a movie. It's kind of a special time because all of your good friends will be there. But you previously agreed to babysit for your little brother twice each month. And your parents want you to babysit on this Saturday night because they have a party they want to attend. Your little brother is nine years old. What will you do?

Describe the strategy you will use to solve this problem on the lines below.

___

What is your solution?

___

44

STRATEGIES FOR PROBLEM SOLVING

You've already listed some strategies for solving problems when you worked on the "party problem." You probably used other strategies to help you solve the problems in Exercise II. The exercise below will help you to see the wide variety of problem solving strategies that are available for you to use.

EXERCISE III

Directions: On the lines below, list all of the strategies for solving problems that you have already thought of in this unit. Look back to Exercises I and II to help you find them.

Then, see if you can think of any other problem solving strategies. If you can, list them also.

_____
_____
_____
_____
_____
_____
_____
_____
_____
_____

SOME FINAL THOUGHTS ABOUT PROBLEM SOLVING

When you are solving problems, try to keep the following ideas in mind:

TAKE YOUR TIME
When you first begin to work on a problem, it's not likely that you'll find an immediate solution. Usually it'll take you some time to find an answer.

DEFINE THE PROBLEM
When you begin to work on a problem, first define just what the problem is.

USE A STRATEGY
Next, think of a couple of strategies that you might be able to use to solve the problem. Pick the best strategy, and go ahead and try it. If it works, you're done! If not, you need to try another one.

USE THE FIVE STEP METHOD
The five step method for solving problems that you have learned in this unit can help you to solve many different kinds of problems.

PAY ATTENTION TO YOUR FEELINGS AND INTUITIONS TOO
Sometimes an organized approach like the five step method doesn't seem right for a problem. In this case, you may have a feeling or an intuition that tells you how to solve the problem. An intuition is something that you know without knowing how you know it: it just pops up in your mind.

Often intuitions and feelings can help you solve problems that more organized methods can't solve. The key is knowing when to follow your intuition and when to use an organized method, like the five steps in this unit. There is no simple way of knowing when to use either. You can only learn from your own experience. For example, your experience would probably tell you to use the five step method for a math problem in your homework. It might also tell you to use an intuition or a feeling to help you solve a problem like the "party problem."

Sometimes you can use an organized method and a feeling or intuition together to help you solve a problem.

UNIT VI SUMMARY: SOLVING PROBLEMS

A problem is any situation in which you have a starting point, a set of directions, and the need to create a solution or answer. The kinds of problems that you are likely to encounter range from problems in math and science to situations in your life outside school, and everything in between.

One way of solving problems is this five step method:

1. Tell yourself exactly what the problem is. Be clear and specific.

2. Think of at least 2-3 possible strategies that you might use to solve the problem. A strategy is a way or method or process for solving a problem. It's not the answer or solution itself but, rather, how you can find the solution or answer.

3. Examine your list of possible strategies, and choose the one that seems best.

4. Try your best strategy, and see if it works to solve the problem. If it works, you're done!

5. If your best strategy doesn't work, go back to your list of possible strategies in Step Two and choose another. Then, try this one.

Or, stop thinking about the problem for awhile, and come back to it later.

Or, research the problem, and then start again with Step Two.

Sometimes following an intuition or a feeling can help you solve a problem more effectively than an organized approach like the five step method can.

UNIT VII
HOW DO YOU STUDY?

INTRODUCTION

In the Introduction to this Program, "studying" was defined as learning for a purpose. You can be studying when you listen, read, watch, talk, think, or do something. In this unit, you are going to look at how you study, particularly when you are doing school work. Also, you will find suggestions that can help you learn to study more effectively.

STUDY ENVIRONMENT

Your environment is everything that surrounds you. Your *study environment,* then, is what surrounds you when you study.

EXERCISE I

Directions: Answer the questions below, and you'll develop a picture of your *study environment.*

1. Where do you usually study at home? _____
   _____

2. What can you see around you when you're studying? _____
   _____

3. What can you hear around you when you're studying? _____
   _____

4. Where do you keep your supplies (books, paper, pens and pencils, etc.) for studying?
   _____

5. Where do you study at school? _____
   _____

6. Is there anywhere else that you study? If so, describe it. _____
   _____

WHAT IS A GOOD STUDY ENVIRONMENT?

People learn in many different ways. We are all individuals and have our own ways of doing things, our own learning styles. So, what is a good study environment for one person may be different from that of another person. However, there do seem to be some parts of a study environment that are good for most people.

EXERCISE II

Directions: What parts of a study environment do you think might be good for most people? On the lines below, list what you think are two parts of a good study environment.

1. _____

2. _____

Description of a Good Study Environment *(from class discussion)*

1. _____
   _____

2. _____
   _____

3. _____
   _____

4. _____
   _____

SUGGESTIONS FOR CREATING A GOOD STUDY ENVIRONMENT

1. Choose a place at home for studying where you feel comfortable, and study in that place. If you have your own room, that's probably the best place. If not, choose a place to study where you will be interrupted by other people as little as possible. Tell your family members about your study place, and ask them to help you by not interrupting you when you are studying.

2. When you study, try to remove things that will distract you. TV is very distracting and will take your attention away from what you're trying to learn. So will a window if you sit in front of one. The fewer distractions you can see, the more effective your learning will probably be.

3. Noise is also a powerful distraction. Try to make your study place as quiet as possible. Ask people not to talk to you when you are studying. If you usually study with music on, try working without it for a week. Give yourself a chance to find out if you can learn better without it.

4. Some people can study even if they are surrounded by distractions. But it takes energy to block them out. When you remove these distractions from your study environment, then you can put that energy into learning. That's why most people can study better in an environment with few or no distractions. When you do remove distractions from your study place, it may take a week or so before you feel comfortable without them and can really see the results. So, give your new study environment a week or two, and then see if it helps you to concentrate and learn. Remember: the key question is, does it help me to study better?

5. If it's hard for you to find a place at home where you can study, ask your family to help you. Tell them that you're trying to study and that you need to reduce the distractions around you as much as possible. Ask them to help you create a good study environment for the time you need to do your work.

If you can't create a good study environment at home, find out when your local library is open. Many people find the library a good place to study. Or, maybe you can study early in the morning before others in your home have awakened.

EXERCISE III

Directions: List two changes you can make in your own study environment that might make it a better place for you to learn.

1. _____

2. _____

EXERCISE IV

Directions: Each of the "stories" below describes one method that a person uses as part of her or his studying. Read each "story," and decide whether you think the method used is good, fair, or poor. Write one of these three words in the blank below each "story."

1. Angela sat down at the table after dinner and started to think about what she had to do for school. "Well," she said to herself, "I have to read three pages about decimals in my math book and then do problems 1-10. For history I have to read the first half of chapter three, the one about the colonies in Virginia and Georgia. Okay, well, the math will take about 45 minutes, and the history will take, oh, maybe half an hour at most. Then I can call up Deirdre or listen to music." She opened her math book and started to read.

   _____

2. Roger opened his science book to page 34 and started to read with the very first word on the page. He was in a hurry, so he didn't bother even to look at the chapter title or any of the headlines. "Gravity is a force..." he read, and his eyes followed the words down the page. But soon, his thoughts began to wander away from what he was reading. "Will I get that job at the market?" he wondered. "And if I don't where else can I find a job close to home?" He decided to ask his mother again if he really had to be home for dinner at 6:30 every night. He read for a few more minutes and then began to think about the new girl in his science class. He liked her sense of humor and wondered if she had noticed him. Ten minutes later he finally finished the first section of the chapter and put the book down on his knee. He wanted to rest for a minute before he went on.

   _____

3. It was ten minutes to nine, and Tony had reached the last page of his history reading. "One more page about the New Deal," he thought, "and I'll be done." The reading wasn't so bad, but he really wanted to watch TV at nine. There was a good football game on. Quickly his eyes raced down the last two columns of print. When he reached the end, he yelled, "Made it!" He tossed the book on his bed, raced into the living room, and turned on the television.

   _____

SUGGESTIONS FOR HOW TO STUDY

1. How do you begin to study?

   Before you start to study, ask yourself what you want to accomplish in this study session. Set goals for how long it might take you to do each part of your work. Be sure that your goals are realistic for you. Also, plan to do your hardest work first when you're most alert.

   Why? If you know what you want to get done and about how long it will take, you can work more efficiently to meet your goals.

Continued on the next page.

2. How do you start an assignment when you want to learn new material?

Quickly tell yourself what you already know about the subject of your assignment. Then, ask yourself questions like the ones below, and answer them.

What do I want to find out about this topic?

What am I trying to learn about it?

Why? Knowing what you are trying to learn will help you to focus more clearly on the material that you are studying. It will help you direct your attention to what is important in that material. It will also help you to keep distracting thoughts out of your mind.

3. What do you do when you finish an assignment?

When you finish studying something, briefly go over what you've just learned. Talk to yourself about it. Imagine that you are explaining it to someone else. Or, actually find another person to whom you can explain what you've learned.

Why? Briefly reviewing what you've just learned will help you to remember it more effectively. A good way to review is to imagine that you're explaining the material to someone else.

EXERCISE V

Directions: Each of the "stories" below and on the next page describes one method that a person uses as part of his or her studying. Beneath each "story" you will find a question about the study method described in that "story."

Read each "story," and answer each question.

1. Dorice liked to work on algebra problems with her friends, Tina and Vanessa. She found that talking about the problems helped her to understand them better. Besides it was a lot more fun than sitting by herself. Tonight, however, she had to write a composition for English. Tina and Vanessa wanted to get together while they were writing. Dorice wanted to go, but she knew that she never got any writing done unless she was alone. Finally she decided to go, but her prediction was right. They spent most of the night talking, and Dorice had to write her composition in a hurry when she got home.

Is there anything Dorice could have done to improve her studying that night?

_____

_____

2. On the second day of school, Lisa had her first homework assignments for the year. "Oh boy," she thought, "they couldn't even wait until next week to start piling it on. This year," she resolved, "I'm going to start my homework right after dinner and get it done then, so I can do what I want to later on. Every night I'll start at the same time," she promised herself.

When she left the table after dinner, Lisa rushed to her room and put her books on the table. But before she began, she decided that she just had to call her friend, Maryann. One call led to another, and then her brother yelled for her to come and watch a show on TV. At 10 o'clock she finally returned to her room and had to rush to do at least some of her homework before she went to sleep.

Is there anything Lisa could have done to improve her studying that night?

_____

_____

3. Tony figured out that he had more than two hours of homework. He knew he'd go crazy if he had to sit still for that long and read and write. He decided to work out a schedule for himself. He would work for half an hour and then relax for 10 minutes. To relax he'd listen to music or talk with someone or something. Then he'd start working again. And he'd keep up that schedule until he had finished his homework.

Is there anything Tony could have done to improve his studying that night?

_____

_____

MORE SUGGESTIONS FOR HOW TO STUDY

1. When is it best to study alone, and when is it good to study with others?

   To answer this question, you have to look carefully at how you learn best. Most people need to study alone when they are reading and writing. Some people like to do problems and study for tests by themselves as well. Others work well with friends and learn a great deal this way. The key is to be aware of what you're really doing when you study. If you're studying with friends and you're getting enough work done, then that method is probably good for you. If you're not getting enough work done, then you need to do more by yourself.

2. When is the best time to study?

   This depends on you. When are you most awake and alert? When can you count on having a study environment without distractions? Try to do your studying at those times. It's helpful for most people to have a definite time for studying and to start working at the same time each day.

   Why? When you start studying at about the same time each day, you can make a habit of it. A habit is something that you do automatically, without a lot of effort. When you make starting to study into a habit, you'll find it much easier to get your work done.

Continued on the next page.

3. How long should you study before taking a break?

For most people, 25-45 minutes is the best length of time for studying before taking a break. Then, rest for 5-15 minutes, or do something you enjoy! If you've studied well, reward yourself. Stretch, walk, talk, listen to music, or do something that you like to do for several minutes. Then, go back to your studying.

Why? When you mix periods of studying with shorter periods of relaxing, you'll be able to pay attention and learn more effectively. The breaks will refresh you and help you come back to your work with new energy.

UNIT VII SUMMARY: HOW DO YOU STUDY?

Your *study environment* is everything that surrounds you when you study. What's in your *study environment* can have an important effect on your learning.

Be aware of your *study environment:*

a. Choose a place at home to study where you feel comfortable, and study in that place.

b. Try to remove as many distractions as you can from your study environment. A distraction is anything that takes your attention away from your studying.

When you are studying, try to use the following methods:

1. Set goals for how much you want to accomplish during each study session. Try to give yourself an idea of how long each assignment will take.

2. When you start an assignment, quickly tell yourself what you already know about it. Then, ask yourself: what am I trying to learn about this? Answer this question.

3. When you finish an assignment, go over what you've just learned. Tell yourself about it as if you were telling another person.

4. Figure out what kinds of studying you do best alone and what you can do well with other people.

5. Find out when you are most awake and alert. Use that time for studying.

6. Try to study for 25-45 minutes at a time. Then, take a break for 5-15 minutes before you start again. Reward yourself during the break by doing something that you enjoy.

UNIT VIII
IMPROVING YOUR MEMORY

A MEMORY GAME

Directions: Below you'll find six different groups of letters. They are lined up in different ways to make it easier for you to concentrate on one group at a time.

Read over group #1 below. Then, cover it with your hand. How many of the letters can you remember? Write all the letters from group #1 that you can remember on the line below that group.

Do the same with groups #2-6.

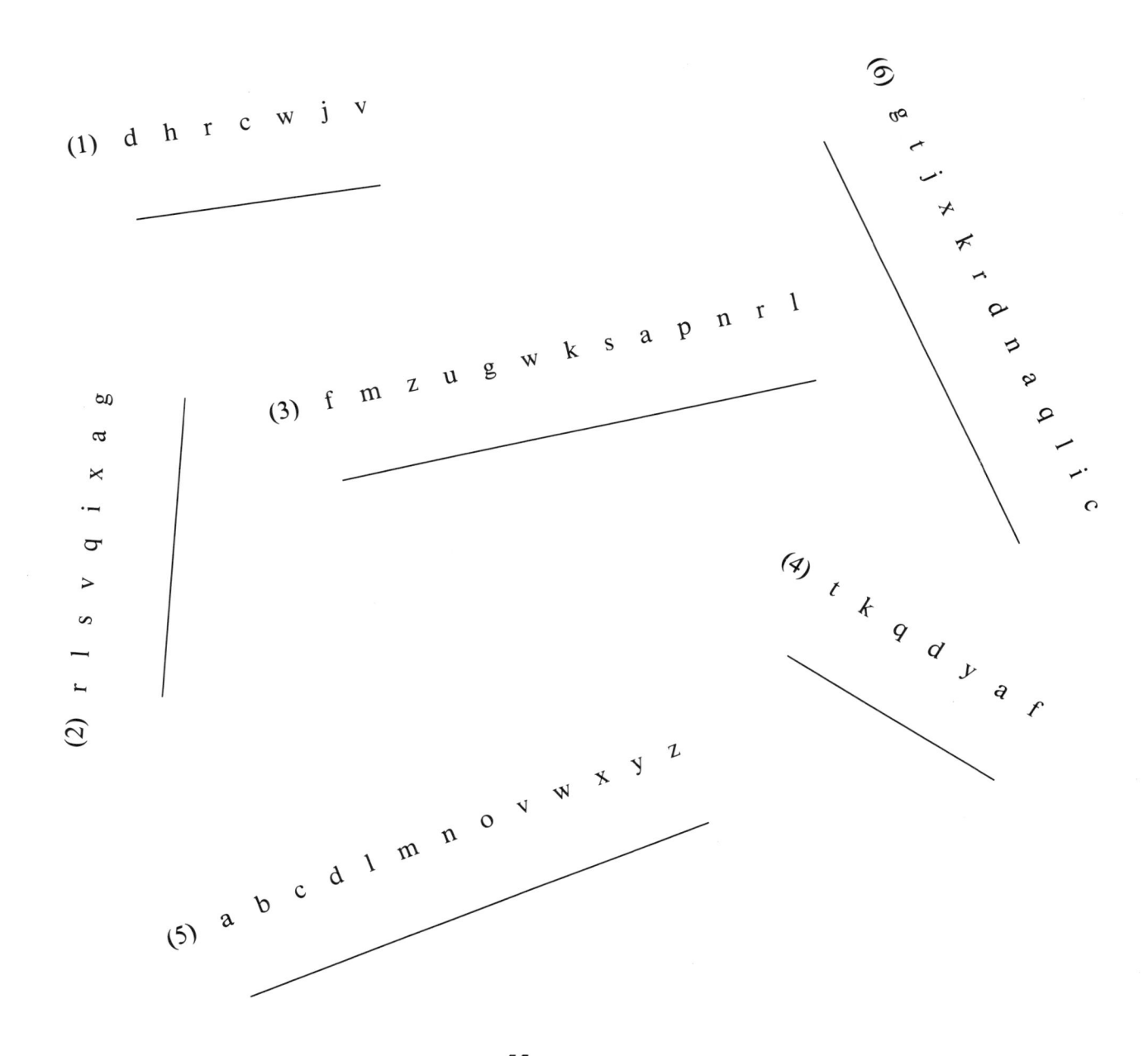

(1) d h r c w j v

(2) r l s v q i x a g

(3) f m z u g w k s a p n r l

(4) t k q d y a f

(5) a b c d l m n o v w x y z

(6) g t j x k r d n a q l i c

LEARNING ABOUT YOUR MEMORY

There are two levels of memory: *short-term memory* and *long-term memory.*

Short-term memory is what you can keep in your attention in the moment. Most people can remember only five to nine different things in their *short-term memories*. That's why you can remember 7 letters easily and 9 letters with a little more difficulty. Yet most people can't remember 10 letters or more.

Long-term memory is what you know and can bring to mind whenever you choose to do so. What is in your *long-term memory* stays with you for a long time. If you review it now and then, you can remember it as long as you like.

You could probably remember the 13 letters in group #5 because this group contains three sequences of letters that are already part of your *long-term memory:* a, b, c, d; l, m, n, o; v, w, x, y, z. To remember this group, you really needed only to remember the first letter in each sequence and the length of the sequence.

ANOTHER MEMORY GAME

Directions: Turn the book so you can read List A. Read List A twice. Then, cover the list with your hand, and write down in the blanks as many words from List A as you can recall.

Next, turn the book so you can read List B. Do the same with List B as you did with List A.

LIST A

pharmacy	heat
spruce	bakery
gas	elm
oak	friction
office	theater
density	maple
fir	hotel
restaurant	

How many words did you correctly recall? _____

LIST B

Birds	Places to play sports	Scientific terms
robin	gym	orbit
sparrow	park	force
hawk	rink	conservation
eagle	pool	phase
crow	field	element

How many words did you correctly recall? _____

WAYS TO REMEMBER

This unit will show you four different ways to remember: grouping, visualizing, repeating, and choosing to remember. Each of these ways can help you to "move" information from short-term memory into long-term memory.

WAYS TO REMEMBER: GROUPING

In "Another Memory Game," you were probably able to remember more of the words in List #2 than in List #1. The words in List #1 were not in any order. The words in List #2 were organized into three groups.

When information is grouped, it is easier to remember. Grouping means to organize information so that details are brought together under the main idea or category that connects them. For example, in "Another Memory Game," each list includes five words that are examples of the category listed in the heading.

Grouping information is one way of helping to "move" it from short-term to long-term memory.

When you want to remember ideas and information, try to organize them into groups that make sense to you. For example, put details with main ideas that they support. List examples with categories that they illustrate. When you group ideas and facts together, remembering one will help you to recall the others.

EXERCISE I

Directions: Think about information that you need to learn and remember for this class that can be grouped in some way.

Write the names of two groups of such information on the top line below. Then, list at least four details or examples for each group.

Details and Examples

Group #1: _____ | Group #2: _____

Details and Examples

WAYS TO REMEMBER: VISUALIZING

Visualizing means to see an image or picture in your mind's eye. For example, close your eyes right now, and see a mental picture of the room in which you are sitting. Try this just for a few seconds. When you see this mental picture, you are visualizing.

Practice visualizing again. Close your eyes and see the face of a friend of yours. Notice how clearly you can see the details of her or his face.

When you want to remember something, visualize a picture of it in your mind. For many people, a mental picture is easier to remember than words are. See as clear an image as you can, and examine it for a few seconds. Then, let it disappear.

One way to use visualizing is to see a mental picture for each main idea that you want to remember. Another way is to see a mental picture of your mapping notes. Many people can remember their mapping notes easily once they have visualized them.

Some people don't visualize clearly. If you don't, you can learn to visualize more clearly by practicing. Look at an object or a picture with your eyes. Then, close your eyes and try to visualize it. The more you practice, the clearer your mental pictures will become.

THE LINK METHOD

Another way that you can use visualizing to help you remember is the link method. The link method is helpful when you need to learn lists of information.

The link method is a mnemonic (ne-mon-ik) method. Mnemonics is the art of training your memory to work more effectively. You'll learn other kinds of mnemonics later in this unit.

On page 60 you'll find directions for using the link method. Read the directions through once. Then, starting with direction #1, follow each direction in the order presented. Use List A to practice the steps of the link method.

List A

1. airplane
2. clown
3. tree
4. rug
5. envelope
6. window
7. pail
8. pen
9. swing
10. chair

Directions:

1. Remember the first word on the list by repeating it several times. Then, picture that word, an airplane, in your mind's eye. Be sure that you see in your mind's eye not the word itself but the object or action that the word stands for.

2. Now, you want to link the first word, "airplane," to the second word, "clown." You can do this in two ways.

    a. One way is to see the first picture that comes to your mind which links these two words. For example: a clown standing next to an airplane.

    b. Another way is to see a ridiculous picture in your mind's eye that links an airplane and a clown. For example: a giant clown standing on his hands on the wings of a flying airplane, or a thousand airplanes buzzing all around a clown as tall as the Washington Monument.

    When you use a ridiculous picture, try to make it really silly. The more ridiculous you can make it, the easier it will be for you to remember.

    How do you make the picture ridiculous?

    — Use action in your picture. Have things moving around or doing something.

    — Change the proportion of how things are usually seen. Make everything larger than life.

    — Use exaggeration. See hundreds or thousands of things.

3. You only need to see the mental picture or image linking the two words for a few seconds. Then, let the picture disappear.

4. Once you've linked the first two words, "airplane" and "clown," go ahead and link the second word, "clown," with the third word, "tree," in the same way. See an image or picture in your mind's eye that includes both a clown and a tree. Choose the first image that comes to mind, or make a ridiculous one.

5. Keep going until you reach the end of the list. Link each word to the one that follows it. For List A, after "airplane" and "clown," and "clown" and "tree," you will link "tree" and "rug," "rug" and "envelope," "envelope" and "window," and so on. In all, you will make nine different images. Remember that you need to see each image or picture only for a few seconds. Then, let that picture disappear.

6. Now that you have linked each word in List A to another one, go back and cover up List A with your hand. How many words from the list can you remember? Write the number of words that you remembered in the space below the list.

EXERCISE II

Directions: Use the link method to learn List B. Remember to follow the steps below:

— Link each word with the one following it in a mental image or picture. Use the first image of the words that comes to mind, or create a ridiculous image of them.

— See each image clearly for a few seconds. Then, let the image disappear.

<u>**List B**</u>

1. basketball
2. lion
3. salami
4. desk
5. star
6. gate
7. nose
8. door
9. truck
10. rock

WAYS TO REMEMBER: REPEATING

Another good way to remember is to repeat information that you want to learn. Be sure to say it in your own words. Even though you've already learned something, go over it one more time. When you repeat information in this way, it will help you move it into your long-term memory and will keep the information available to you.

One good way to repeat information is to say it aloud to yourself. When you say it aloud, not only do you speak the information but you also hear it.

WAYS TO REMEMBER: CHOOSING TO REMEMBER

You can always remember more effectively when you choose to remember. The more that you want to learn and know, the more you'll be able to remember what you have learned.

To choose to remember, you need to pay attention to and be interested in what you are learning.

MNEMONICS

As explained above, mnemonic methods are ways of remembering more efficiently. The link method is an example of one. Another mnemonic is the rhyme below:

"Thirty days has September,
April, June and November."

Two other mnemonic methods are acronyms and acrostics.

ACRONYMS

An acronym is a word that is made by taking the first letter from each word that you want to remember and making a new word from all of those letters. For example, if you wanted to remember how to make mental pictures ridiculous when you use the link method, you could learn the acronym *ape* from the words action, proportion, and exaggeration.

EXERCISE III

Directions: Try to create acronyms for remembering the two groups of information below. Write each acronym on the line below the information that it represents.

1. The Great Lakes: Superior, Huron, Michigan, Erie, Ontario.

    Hint: you can put the names of the lakes in any helpful order.

    _____

2. The colors of visible light in the spectrum and the order in which they appear: red, orange, yellow, green, blue, indigo, violet.

    Hint: an acronym can be more than one word.

    _____

EXERCISE IV

Directions: Sometimes acronyms are used so frequently that people begin to treat them as if they were words. Do you know the meanings of the acronyms listed below? Write the meaning of each acronym below on the lines provided.

1. awol _____

2. snafu _____

3. Nato _____

EXERCISE V

Directions: Can you create any acronyms that can help you remember information that you need to know? List any acronyms that you can create on the lines below.

_____

_____

_____

ACROSTICS

An acrostic is a sentence that is made by taking the first letter from each word or symbol that you want to remember and then inserting another word beginning with the same letter. For example, to help you remember the lines on a musical staff, the acrostic is: Every good boy does fine.

E — Every
G — good
B — boy
D — does
F — fine.

Another useful acrostic can help you remember the classification system of living things in biology: King Phillip came over for green stamps.

Kingdom — K — King
Phylum — P — Phillip
Class — C — came
Order — O — over
Family — F — for
Genus — G — green
Species — S — stamps

Do you know any acrostics that have been useful to you?

OTHER MNEMONIC METHODS

There are many other mnemonic methods, for example, peg words and "shopping lists." These other mnemonics include methods for remembering names and numbers, errands and appointments, and other kinds of information.

If you want to learn more about mnemonic methods, find a book about memory in your school or public library that will explain them to you. Then, all you need to do is practice. (One good book about memory is *The Memory Book,* by Harry Lorayne and Jerry Lucas.)

UNIT VIII SUMMARY: IMPROVING YOUR MEMORY

There are two levels of memory: short-term memory and long-term memory.

— Short-term memory is what you can keep in your attention in the moment. Most people can only remember five to nine different things in their short-term memories.

— Long-term memory is what you know and can bring to mind whenever you choose to do so.

An important part of learning is "moving" information from your short-term memory into your long-term memory. Four ways to accomplish this are:

1. Grouping information

    To group information is to organize it so that details are brought together under the main idea or category that connects them.

2. Visualizing information

    To visualize information is to see an image or picture of it in your mind's eye. For example, you can see a mental picture of an idea or event or an image of your mapping notes.

3. Repeating information

    To repeat information is to put the information in your own words and go over it. Say it aloud to yourself so that you can hear it as well as speak it.

4. Choosing to remember

    The more you choose to remember, the more you will remember. To choose to remember, you need to want to pay attention to and be interested in what you are learning.

Mnemonics is the art of remembering. Mnemonic methods are ways of remembering more efficiently. Three useful mnemonic methods are:

1. The link method

    Link each word in a list with the one following it by creating a picture or image in your mind's eye in which you see objects or events representing both words.

2. Acronym

    An acronym is a word that is made by taking the first letter from each word that you want to remember and making a new word from all of those letters.

3. Acrostic

    An acrostic is a sentence that is made by taking the first letter from each word or symbol that you want to remember and inserting another word beginning with that same letter.

UNIT IX

ORGANIZING THE PARAGRAPH

THE PARAGRAPH DETECTIVE (PART I)

Directions: Each of the two paragraphs below has one major error or weakness in the way it is written. Read each paragraph carefully, and briefly describe what you think is wrong with it. Write your descriptions on the lines below the paragraphs.

A. (1) It developed from a mixture of country-western music, played by whites, and black rhythm and blues. (2) Teenagers first heard the records on the radio, liked the lively beat of the music, and started to buy them. (3) One of the biggest attractions of the new music was the way people could dance to it. (4) The performers were mostly young men in their late teens and early twenties, people like Chuck Berry, Little Richard, Bill Haley, and Buddy Holly. (5) The singer who became the most famous and successful was Elvis Presley, who was a genuine sensation for many years. (6) By the end of the 1950's, he had sold $120 million worth of records.

_____

_____

_____

B. (1) Many people don't like cold winters, but I think they're great because of all the winter sports I enjoy. (2) Where we live, winter starts in November and lasts at least until March. (3) Often the temperature stays below the freezing point for weeks on end. (4) When that happens all of the ponds and streams freeze over with a thick layer of ice. (5) Also, when snow falls, it usually stays around until spring comes to melt it away.

_____

_____

_____

WHAT IS A PARAGRAPH?

The first basic building block of good writing is the *complete sentence*. The second one is the *paragraph*.

A paragraph is a group of sentences that are organized around *one* main idea and that work together to explain, describe, or discuss that idea.

REMEMBER: A good paragraph has *one* main idea.

Once you've learned to write good paragraphs, you have the key skill to do any kind of writing that you will ever want to do.

WHAT ARE THE ELEMENTS OF A GOOD PARAGRAPH?

A. TOPIC SENTENCE

A *topic sentence* is a sentence that clearly tells the reader what the paragraph is about. It expresses the main idea or topic of the paragraph. Usually it's the first sentence in the paragraph. (Look at the Example Paragraph on page 67. The first sentence is the topic sentence.)

EXERCISE I

Directions: On the lines below, write a good topic sentence for paragraph A on page 65.

_____

_____

_____

B. SUPPORT

The topic sentence gives the main idea of the paragraph. All of the other sentences in the paragraph should give details and examples that describe, back up, or explain the main idea. This giving of details and examples is called *support*. In the Example Paragraph on page 67, see how all of the sentences tell you more about the topic sentence.

EXAMPLE PARAGRAPH

Working as a golf caddy is the best job I've ever had. I've met a lot of interesting people and have also learned a great deal about the game of golf. Once I actually had the chance to caddy for a pro who has won five major tournaments. Caddying is always outdoor work which I really appreciate, particularly on beautiful summer days. The job provides me with a lot of exercise, too. Walking the golf course several times a day can easily add up to 20 miles or more. Finally, the pay is good, and there are some excellent fringe benefits, like tips and gifts of old golf equipment.

EXERCISE II

Directions: Write two sentences that give *support* to the topic sentence in paragraph B on page 65.

1. _____

2. _____

THE PARAGRAPH DETECTIVE (Part II)

Directions: Each of the two paragraphs below has *one* major error or weakness in the way it is written. Read each paragraph carefully, and briefly describe what you think is wrong with it. Write your descriptions on the lines below the paragraphs.

C. (1) I first learned to like camping in the mountains during the summer I worked in Wyoming. (2) Every Friday afternoon while I was there, Mr. Crenshaw would drive me and at least one of the other guys up to the end of High Valley Road. (3) You might have seen that road on TV because they once filmed a cigarette commercial up there with a lot of fake cowboys. (4) Then we'd hike in following the Little Muddy Creek Trail until we reached the shores of Beaver Lake. (5) It was a tough climb at first, particularly with a full pack on my back. (6) My pack is a Gerry Mountaineer, green with red stripes. (7) But as the summer went on, I got used to the weight and became a better climber as well. (8) After about three hours of climbing, we'd reach the lake and make camp. (9) Then we would have that night, all day Saturday, and Sunday morning before we had to climb back down to the road. (10) The time I spent up there in the mountains swimming, hiking around, cooking my own food, and just being alone in the wilderness was the best part of my summer. (11) I like hot dogs and beans a lot.

_____
_____
_____

D. (1) There are many ways to bake bread, but the method I use is called the No Failure Method because you can't go wrong if you follow the directions. (2) First you mix the yeast, honey, milk, water, and half the flour. (3) Beat this mixture together well, and then let it rise in a warm place for one hour. (4) Then you add the oil and the other half of the flour. (5) Roll the dough into a ball, and knead it for at least 10 minutes. (6) Let it rise twice, each time for another hour. (7) Then fashion the dough into loaves, and bake them at 350 degrees for 45 minutes. (8) When you knead the dough, make sure you work it all together thoroughly. (9) Don't put in too much oil, or the bread will taste greasy. (10) Be sure to use water and milk that's warm but not hot to the touch.

_____
_____
_____

WHAT ARE THE ELEMENTS OF A GOOD PARAGRAPH? (cont.)

C. UNITY

The word *unity* means oneness, that different things are all part of the same larger whole. *Unity* in a paragraph means that all of the ideas and information in that paragraph are directly related to the main idea expressed in the topic sentence. (The Example Paragraph on page 67 has unity. It is a *unified* paragraph.)

EXERCISE III

Directions: On the line below, write the numbers of the sentences in paragraph C on page 68 that are not in *unity* with the rest of the paragraph.

D. COHERENCE

The word *coherence* means sticking together. In a paragraph, *coherence* means that each sentence should "stick" to the sentence that comes before it; that is, each sentence should follow the previous one in a way that makes sense. (The Example Paragraph on page 67 has *coherence*. It is a *coherent* paragraph.)

EXERCISE IV

Directions: On the line below, write the numbers of the sentences in paragraph D on page 68 that are not *coherent* with the rest of the paragraph.

A WAY TO ORGANIZE PARAGRAPHS

Writing good paragraphs begins with organizing your ideas. This is a skill that you can learn. The method of organizing your ideas described below can help you to express your ideas and feelings in writing more clearly and effectively.

Here are six steps for organizing a paragraph.

1. First, *think* about what you want to say. Ask yourself: what are the ideas and/or feelings that I want to communicate?

2. Ask yourself: what is the *main idea* of this paragraph? Think about what the possibilities are. Then, decide what the *main idea* is and jot it down on a piece of paper.

3. Write down a few words about each detail and example that you want to include in the paragraph. This will give you an *outline* from which to write.

    Example Outlines

    (A) main idea
      1. detail
      2. detail
      3. detail

    (B) why take vacations in Canada
      1. mountains — climbing, skiing
      2. lakes — swimming, boating
      3. big cities — Toronto, Montreal, Vancouver
      4. French Canadian culture — Quebec

Or, you can write down your ideas and examples in *mapping* form.

Example of Mapping

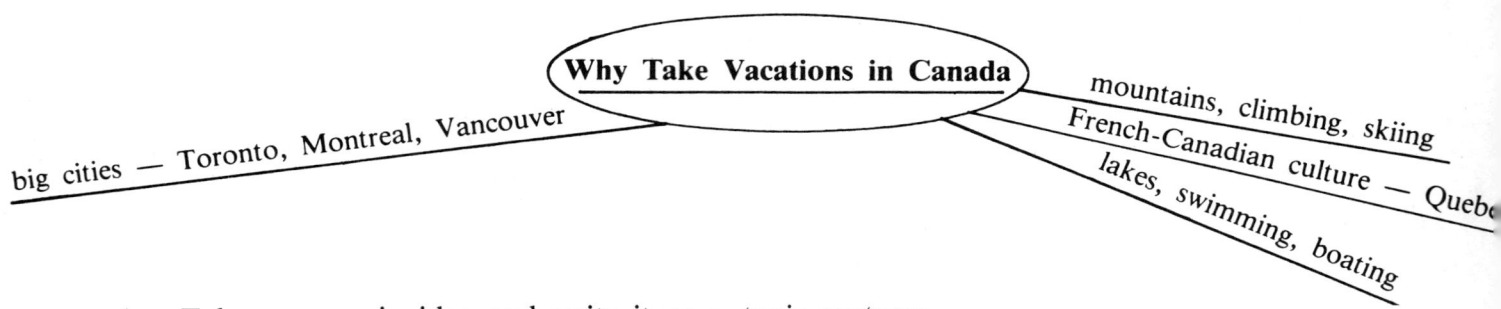

Why Take Vacations in Canada
- big cities — Toronto, Montreal, Vancouver
- mountains, climbing, skiing
- French-Canadian culture — Quebec
- lakes, swimming, boating

4. Take your main idea and write it as a *topic sentence*.

    Example of a Topic Sentence

    There are many good reasons for taking your vacation in Canada.

5. Then, write the rest of your paragraph, working from the outline that you made before. Be sure to include all the details and examples from your outline in your paragraph.

6. Read over what you've written and check for *support, unity,* and *coherence.* If your paragraph doesn't say what you want it to say, rewrite it.

EXERCISE V

Directions: Write an outline for a paragraph describing what you think you'll be like when you're 21 years old. Include at least *three* details that support your main idea.

main idea _____

_____

supporting detail 1. _____

_____

supporting detail 2. _____

_____

supporting detail 3. _____

_____

supporting detail 4. _____

_____

supporting detail 5. _____

_____

supporting detail 6. _____

_____

UNIT IX SUMMARY: ORGANIZING THE PARAGRAPH

The two basic building blocks of good writing are the complete sentence and the paragraph.

A paragraph is a group of sentences that are organized around one main idea.

The elements of a good paragraph are:

1. Topic sentence — A sentence that clearly states what the paragraph is about, usually placed at the beginning of the paragraph.

2. Support — Details and examples that describe, back up, or explain the topic sentence.

3. Unity — All of the sentences are directly related to the main idea expressed in the topic sentence.

4. Coherence — Each sentence follows the one before it in a way that makes sense.

Writing good paragraphs begins with organizing your ideas. You can use the method described below to organize your ideas before you write, and then write a paragraph.

1. First, think about what you want to say.

2. Write down the main idea of the paragraph. Then, jot down the details and examples that you want to include under it. This will give you a working outline.

3. Take your main idea and write it as a topic sentence. Then, using your outline as a guide, write the rest of the paragraph.

4. Read over what you've written and check for support, unity, and coherence.

UNIT X
PREPARING FOR AND TAKING TESTS: OBJECTIVE QUESTIONS

HOW DO YOU PREPARE FOR A TEST?

Think about how you prepare for a test. What do you do to get ready before you take the test? What kinds of resources do you use to study? And how do you use them? How much time do you give to preparing for a test? Do you study alone or with others?

Imagine that you will have a whole period test in this class a week from today. On the lines below, briefly describe how you'd prepare for it.

_____

_____

_____

_____

_____

PREPARING FOR A TEST

How you prepare for a test has a lot to do with how well you'll do on it. Later in this unit, you'll read some ideas about how you can better prepare for tests. Then, you'll be asked to think about these ideas in relation to what you've described above.

TEST QUESTIONS

There are two things that determine how well you will do on a test. One is what you know. This is the result of how well you have learned during the class and how you have prepared for the test.

The other is how well you understand how to answer test questions. The more that you understand about how test questions work, the better you'll be able to show what you do know in answering those questions.

There are two kinds of test questions that you will be asked to answer in high school. These are objective questions and essay questions. This unit will deal with objective questions. Unit XI will deal with essay questions.

WHAT ARE OBJECTIVE QUESTIONS?

Objective questions usually try to find out if you know facts or other kinds of specific information. They may also test more general understandings and skills. Usually, for an objective question, there is only one correct answer for which you will receive credit.

Objective questions often do not require much writing in their answers. You may be asked to write a word or two in a blank or even a few sentences. Frequently, objective questions only ask you to pick a word, a letter, or number that represents the answer. On a standardized test, you may be asked to fill in a blank square or circle next to the correct answer.

The most commonly used kinds of objective questions are:

1. MULTIPLE CHOICE
2. MATCHING
3. SHORT ANSWER
4. TRUE/FALSE

WHAT CAN YOU LEARN ABOUT OBJECTIVE QUESTIONS THAT WILL BE HELPFUL?

There are methods you can learn to use that will help you in answering each kind of objective question. These methods are not a substitute for preparing for the test by learning the material on which you'll be tested. However, they can help you use what you do know more effectively when you're taking a test.

On the next pages you'll find a method or methods for answering each kind of objective question.

MULTIPLE CHOICE

Multiple choice questions ask you to choose the right answer from a number of possible answers. This is one of the most frequently used kinds of questions, and it can be tricky, even when you know the right answer. The method described below is one good way to go about answering multiple choice questions.

How To Answer Multiple Choice Questions

1. First, read the question carefully.

2. Try to anticipate the answer in your mind before you start to look at the choices. When you can anticipate the answer and find it among the choices, it's likely to be correct.

3. Read the choices given, and try to find the right answer.

4. Even if you're sure that the first or second choice is correct, read over all of the other choices just to be certain. They may all be correct, and the last choice may be "all of the above."

5. If you don't know which choice is correct after you've read all of them, try this:

    Use a process of elimination. First, cross off all of the choices that you know to be wrong. Often this will leave you with only two possible choices left. Pick the one that you think is best.

    If you have no idea which choice is correct, guess (unless there is a penalty for guessing). Guessing can't hurt your score, and you might guess the correct answer.

Example

When people are in high school, they are
(A) 18   (B) 16   (C) 15   (D) 17
(E) all of the above   years old.

EXERCISE I

Directions: Answer each of the following questions by writing the letter of the correct answer in the blank at the right.

1. How many states have capital cities?
   (A) 50   (B) 48   (C) half
   (D) most   (E) a lot   _____

2. Anyone born in the United States of America and over 35 years of age can legally be
   (A) an American citizen   (B) a doctor
   (C) male or female   (D) President
   (E) all of the above   _____

3. Human beings are, according to taxonomic groupings:
   (A) insects   (B) crustaceans
   (C) animals   (D) plants
   (E) none of the above   _____

4. People first started to watch a lot of television in
   (A) 1899   (B) the 1950s   (C) 1776
   (D) the 1920s   (E) 1964.   _____

5. The best method to use in answering multiple choice questions is to
   (A) guess a lot
   (B) pick the first answer that seems right
   (C) read through all of the choices and pick the best one
   (D) start with the last question and work backwards
   (E) none of the above.   _____

Narrowing Down The Choices

How do you narrow down the choices when you use a process of elimination? Multiple choice questions often give you information in the question itself that can help you narrow down the choices. You need to figure out (1) what information is given in the question, and (2) how you can use it.

For example, read the question below.

> Anne Hutchinson was driven from the Massachusetts Bay Colony because she taught people:
>
> (A) to live by the Golden Rule
> (B) how to buy a good used car
> (C) survival skills in desert climates
> (D) to stand up for their beliefs, come what may

The question itself tells you that (1) Anne Hutchinson was living in the Massachusetts Bay Colony (2) in colonial times, that is, before 1776, and (3) that she was driven from there because of her teachings. With this information, you can begin to narrow down the choices in terms of:

1. Historical probability: Could it have happened at this place, in this time? (This is particularly useful on social studies tests.)

2. Common sense: Is the answer reasonable? Or, is it silly or foolish?

EXERCISE II

Directions: Narrow down the choices in the question on page 77 about Anne Hutchinson. On the line to the right, write the letters of the choices that you can eliminate because they are foolish or historically unlikely. _____

Now, use the same "narrowing down" method for questions 1-4 below. Draw a line through the letter before each choice that you eliminate.

1. George Washington's false teeth were made of
   (A) soap   (B) plastic   (C) iron   (D) wood   (E) aluminum foil

2. If both the President and the Vice President of the United States were to die, who would become President?
   (A) the Speaker of the House
   (B) the governor of California
   (C) Abraham Lincoln   (D) the Queen of England
   (E) the Commissioner of the National Football League

3. Most people in the United States commute to work on
   (A) airplanes   (B) buses and trains   (C) boats
   (D) cars   (E) bicycles

4. The kangaroo's pouch helps it to
   (A) protect its young
   (B) store food
   (C) take fewer but longer trips
   (D) all of the above

MATCHING

Matching questions usually give you two lists of information and ask you to connect them with each other in some way.

When you answer a matching question, first read the directions carefully. Then, use a process of elimination to answer the question, as follows:

1. Complete the matches that you know first, and cross them off.

2. Then, do the best you can with whichever words are left in each column. If you're not sure, guess (unless there is a penalty for guessing).

Example

Directions: Write the number of each animal in the blank to the left of the word which names a part of that animal.

1.	dog	_____	hands
2.	opossum	_____	spinnerets
3.	horse	_____	wings
4.	spider	_____	paws
5.	bird	_____	mane
6.	human	_____	pouch

EXERCISE III

Directions: Write the number of each city in the blank to the left of the state in which that city is located.

1.	Chicago	_____	Maine
2.	New York	_____	Texas
3.	Boise	_____	Louisiana
4.	Tulsa	_____	Illinois
5.	Baton Rouge	_____	California
6.	Bangor	_____	Idaho
7.	Amarillo	_____	New York
8.	Ukiah	_____	Oklahoma

SHORT ANSWER

With short answer questions, you need to know the answer. There are no choices given to you. However, if you don't know the exact answer but do know something related to it, write down what you do know. You may get partial credit for it. Also, guess if you don't know the answer (unless there is a penalty for guessing).

EXERCISE IV

Directions: Fill in the blank with the right answer.

1. There are _____ whole numbers between one and ten, not including one or ten.

2. How did the first Europeans get to America?
   _____

3. People in Great Britain drive on the _____ side of the road.

TRUE/FALSE

True/false questions are statements that you are asked to judge. Are they true or false?

True/false questions may seem easy, but they can also be very tricky and difficult. The single most important point to remember in doing these questions is this: for a statement to be true, it must be entirely true.

Be careful with statements that have one true part and one false part. IF ANY PART OF A STATEMENT IS FALSE, THEN IT IS A FALSE STATEMENT.

Also, be careful with statements that include the words all, always, only, or never. They are often false.

Example

Directions: Write true or false in the blank following each statement according to your judgment of its truth.

1. All statements that have the word "never" in them are false. _____

2. The sun is bigger than the moon, and the moon is bigger than the earth. _____

EXERCISE V

Directions: Each of the 12 statements below deals with suggestions for preparing to take tests or for taking objective tests. Read them carefully. Then, mark them "T" for true or "F" for false.

1. It is helpful to know what kind of test your teacher is going to give you. _____

2. Teachers almost never give clues beforehand about what's going to be on a test. _____

3. People learn most efficiently by studying for one long period of time the night before a test. _____

4. The best way to study is to re-read your notes and assignments. _____

5. It's very helpful to try to anticipate what questions your teacher will ask you on the test and then tell yourself the answers to those questions when you're studying. _____

6. A good way to prepare for a test is to watch the late show with your friends and eat breakfast in the morning. _____

7. Students who worry a lot about tests always do better. _____

8. You should begin to answer the first question on the test right after you read it. _____

9. Read all the directions on the test carefully. Then, follow them exactly. _____

10. Guess whenever you don't know the answer unless there's a penalty for guessing. _____

11. Do the hardest questions first. That way you'll get the hardest questions out of the way. _____

12. Don't second guess yourself when going over your answers. Trust your first judgment unless new information comes up. _____

ANSWERS FOR EXERCISE V: TRUE/FALSE QUESTIONS

Suggestions For Preparing For Tests

1. TRUE — Yes, it's very helpful to know what kind of test you are going to have. If you know what kind of test you'll have, you'll be better able to study for it.

2. FALSE — Not true! Teachers often give clues about what they think is most important, and what they think is important is usually what you'll need to know for a test. Pay close attention to what the teacher says in the classes just before the test.

3. FALSE — No, people don't learn best this way. You can learn more by studying for several shorter periods of time rather than one long one. If possible, study for some time on each of the several days before the test. Don't wait until the last night to begin to study.

4. FALSE — Don't just re-read! When you study, ask yourself questions about the material and then answer them. If you can't answer them, then look up the answer. Study actively!

5. TRUE — Yes! Try to anticipate what questions your teacher will ask you, and then tell yourself the answers. You'll be surprised at how good you can get at this!

6. FALSE — Get a good night's sleep before a test. Be as physically ready as you would be for a sporting event. However, it does help most people to eat breakfast before they take a test.

7. FALSE — Not true! Worrying won't help you. When you study and when you take the test, try to relax. Don't worry; do the best you can!

Suggestions For Taking Objective Tests

8. FALSE   No, don't start answering right away. First, look over the entire test. Know how much time you have to finish it, and how much time you want to give to each question or set of questions.

9. TRUE   Yes! Read all directions carefully; follow them exactly.

10. TRUE   Yes! Guessing can't hurt your score, unless there's a penalty for guessing. And you may guess the right answer!

11. FALSE   No, don't do the hardest questions first. Rather, do the questions you know best first. Also, if you don't know the answer to a question, don't spend a lot of time puzzling over it. Go on to the next questions, and come back to the difficult one later if you have time.

12. TRUE   Yes! When going over your answers, trust your first judgment unless new information comes up to convince you that your first answer is wrong. Don't second guess yourself.

EXERCISE VI

Directions: Think about the suggestions for preparing for a test listed on page 82. Then, go back and re-read what you wrote on page 73 about how you get ready for a test.

On the lines below, briefly describe two new ways of preparing for a test that you'd be interested in trying.

_____

_____

_____

_____

_____

_____

UNIT X SUMMARY: PREPARING FOR AND TAKING TESTS: OBJECTIVE QUESTIONS

Objective questions usually have one correct answer for which you will receive credit.

There are four main kinds of objective questions. You can learn methods for answering them that will help you on a test.

The four main kinds of objective questions are:

1. Multiple Choice — Read the question carefully. Try to think of the answer before you look at the choices. Read all of the choices given. If you don't know the answer after you've read the choices, use a process of elimination. Cross off the choices you know to be wrong. Pick the most sensible one that remains. When you can, use information in the question itself to help you narrow down the choices.

2. Matching — Do the ones you know first, and cross them off. Then, do the best you can with whatever ones are left.

3. Short Answer — If you don't know the exact answer, write down anything you do know that's related. You may get partial credit.

4. True/False — Read the statements very carefully. Remember that all parts of a statement must be true for the statement to be true.

How you prepare for a test has a lot to do with how well you'll do on it. The more skillfully you prepare, the better you'll do.

UNIT XI
PREPARING FOR AND TAKING TESTS: ESSAY QUESTIONS

ANSWERING ESSAY QUESTIONS

The method you learned in Unit IX for organizing a paragraph is also effective when you answer an essay question on a test. Do you know the steps in this method? If not, turn to page 70 and look over this method again.

As you work through this unit, you'll see how you can use this method to help you answer essay questions.

WHAT IS AN ESSAY QUESTION?

An essay question asks you to write a composition of at least one paragraph and often several paragraphs during the test time itself.

An essay question usually asks you to organize what you know and understand about a topic and then to express it in a way that responds to that particular question.

Most essay questions focus on ideas and understandings, not on facts. Yet, you need to include facts in your essay answers when the facts are supporting details that prove your points.

Three examples of essay questions

1. Explain the process of river erosion.

2. Compare and contrast the two main characters in *The Outsiders* by S. E. Hinton.

3. Discuss the United States' space program in the 1960s and how it affected our lives.

A METHOD FOR WRITING ANSWERS TO ESSAY QUESTIONS

Before The Test

1. When your teacher schedules a test, find out whether the test will include essay questions. You can answer these questions more efficiently when you prepare for them in advance.

2. When you study, try to anticipate the essay questions that your teacher will ask. Ask yourself: what does he or she think is really important in this chapter or unit? How will he or she ask about this?

   Then, think about how you would answer the essay questions you have posed. Tell yourself the answers you would write. If you need to look anything up to complete these answers, be sure to do that. You'll be surprised at how good you can get at figuring out the questions ahead of time.

When You First Get The Test

1. When you first get the test, read the directions carefully. If you have a choice of essay questions, read all of the questions first. Then, choose the ones you can best answer.

2. Some tests tell you how much each question is worth. If possible, plan to give a certain amount of time to each question based both on how much that question is worth and how well you think you can answer it.

3. Start by working on the question that you can do best (but be careful not to spend too much time on it). This will help to get you thinking about the material on the test and build your confidence.

REMEMBER: Spending a minute or two in planning your time when you have several essays to write is well worth it. Planning your time in this way can help you make sure that you answer all of the questions or, at least, those that will benefit you the most.

How To Organize Your Essay

1. To write an essay on a test, you can use exactly the same method you used to organize and write a paragraph. You'll have to work more quickly on a test, but you can follow the same steps, as listed below:

   a. Read the question carefully. Then, think about what you want to say in response to the question.

   b. Jot down a brief outline of your answer.

   c. Then, write your answer.

   d. If you have time, read over your essay and make any necessary changes or corrections.

2. The purpose of writing an outline, as noted in step b above, is to help you organize your answer. When you jot down your outline, try to list all of the main ideas and important details that you want to include in your answer. At the same time, try to keep your outline brief.

   You'll find an example of an outline for an answer to an essay question below. The essay question is: "Discuss the United States' space program in the 1960s and how it affected our lives."

   Example of Outline

   I. U.S. space program in 60s
      A. Stimulated by competition with Russians
      B. Unmanned rockets first
      C. Astronauts in orbit around Earth
      D. 1969 — landing on moon

   II. How it affected our lives
      A. Excitement about space
      B. New technology — computers, teflon, etc.
      C. Satellites — weather forecasting, etc.
      D. Interest in space stations

EXERCISE I

Directions: Read the essay question below. Think about the question, and decide how you'd like to answer it. Then, outline your answer on the lines beneath the question.

QUESTION: Describe why the place where you live either is or is not a good place to live.

How To Begin Writing Your Essay

The best way to begin an essay answer is with a *thesis statement*. A *thesis statement* is a sentence that gives the main ideas of your answer. It's like a topic sentence for your answer.

For example, a *thesis statement* for an answer in response to the question on page 87 about the U.S. space program might be:

> The United States' space program in the 1960s moved quickly through several different stages, from tiny, unmanned capsules to a landing on the moon, and had many important effects on our lives.

Sometimes you can rephrase the essay question itself and use it as part of your thesis statement. For example, the beginning of a *thesis statement* in an answer to the question in Exercise I might be:

> The place where I live is a good place because . . .

When you rephrase the question in this way, you can be sure that you are starting on target with your answer.

How To Use Your Time

Try to divide the time you give to each essay question in the following way:

Thinking and outlining	15–30%
Writing the essay	60–75%
Reading over and correcting your essay	10–15%

For example, if you have 20 minutes to answer an essay question, you could divide your time as follows:

Thinking and outlining	5 minutes
Writing the essay	13 minutes
Reading over and correcting your essay	2 minutes

REMEMBER: When a teacher grades an essay, more does not mean better. A shorter but well-organized and well-written essay will convey your understanding more effectively to your teacher. This kind of essay will almost always earn a higher grade than a longer one which is sloppy and disorganized.

WHAT WORDS ARE USED TO ASK ESSAY QUESTIONS?

Essay questions usually begin with or include a key word that tells you what kind of answer is expected. You need to know what this key word means to answer the question well.

Below you'll find a list of words often used to ask essay questions. Your teacher will help you to understand the meanings of these words.

1. describe _____

2. summarize _____

3. compare _____

4. contrast _____

5. explain _____

6. evaluate _____

7. criticize _____

8. discuss _____

MORE SUGGESTIONS FOR WRITING ESSAY ANSWERS

1. Be sure to include both main ideas and supporting details in your answer. The main ideas show that you understand the meaning of the question. The supporting details help to prove the main idea.

2. Stick to your topic as you write. Only answer what the question asks. Don't put in all you know about the subject unless the question calls for that. Writing a brief outline first will help you stick to your topic.

3. If you don't know the entire answer to a question you are working on, start writing what you do know. You may earn partial credit, and the rest of the answer may come to you as you write.

4. Answer in outline form if you lack the time to write out your answer as an essay. Your teacher may give you partial credit for showing what you know about the question.

WHAT CAN YOU DO WHEN A TEST IS RETURNED TO YOU?

There are several ways that you can learn from a test your teacher has corrected and returned to you. Can you name two of these ways?

1. _____
   _____

2. _____
   _____

UNIT XI SUMMARY: PREPARING FOR AND TAKING TESTS: ESSAY QUESTIONS

An essay question asks you to organize what you know and understand about a topic and to express it in a way that responds to that particular question. You need to organize your essay answer around main ideas and include important details that support these main ideas.

You can use the same method for organizing and writing your answer to an essay question that you used for writing paragraphs. You'll need to work more quickly when you're taking a test, but the method is well worth using.

Below are the steps in the method:

1. Read the essay question carefully. Then, think about what you want to say in response to the question.

2. Jot down a brief outline of your answer.

3. Begin your essay answer with a thesis statement that states the main ideas of your answer. A thesis statement is like a topic sentence for your answer.

4. Then, write your answer.

5. If you have time, read over your essay and make any necessary changes or corrections.

To answer essay questions well, you need to understand the special words that teachers use to ask these questions. Some of these words are: describe, summarize, compare, contrast, explain, evaluate, criticize, and discuss.

UNIT XII
USING YOUR TIME

ASSIGNMENT BEFORE CLASS

Directions: On the lines on page 94, write down everything that you do during the course of one average school day. Also, write the time of day of each activity and how much time you give to each activity.

See the "Sample Record Of A School Day" on page 95 for an example of how to do this.

Keep track of the following:

1. The time of day that you began the activity

2. The type of activity

3. The amount of time given to each activity

RECORD OF A SCHOOL DAY

Date _____   Day of the week _____

TIME OF DAY   ACTIVITY   LENGTH OF TIME

LEARNING FROM YOUR RECORD OF SCHOOL DAY

Directions: Answer the questions below.

1. Examine your "Record" to find out how much time you gave to each of the kinds of activities listed below. Write the amount of time given to each kind of activity on the space to the right of that activity.

   In school _____   Jobs _____   Homework _____   Activities _____

   Sports _____   TV _____   Being with friends _____

   Meals _____   Relaxing/free time _____   On the phone _____

   Other _____

2. Looking at your record, do you see any use of time that surprises you? Do you see any use of time that you'd like to change? If so, what?

   _____
   _____
   _____
   _____

SAMPLE RECORD OF A SCHOOL DAY

TIME OF DAY	ACTIVITY	LENGTH OF TIME
7:15 AM	Wake up	
7:20	Breakfast, get ready for school	40 minutes
8:00	Walk to school	30 minutes
8:30	In school	6 hours
2:30 PM	Club meeting in school	50 minutes
3:20	Talk to friends	30 minutes
3:50	Walk home	30 minutes
4:20	Listen to music, talk on phone	1 hour, 10 minutes
5:30	Clean room, help with younger children	40 minutes
6:10	Dinner	40 minutes
6:50	Do dishes	25 minutes
7:15	Do homework	1 hour, 45 minutes
9:00	Watch TV	1 hour, 30 minutes
10:30	Talk with sister	25 minutes
11:00	Go to sleep	

INTRODUCTION

One useful study skill that can help you as much as any other is learning how to use your time well. A method that many people use to organize the way they use their time is a *schedule*. A *schedule* is a plan that you create for how you want to spend your time. First, you figure out what you *need* and *want* to do. Then, you give a certain amount of time in your schedule to each activity.

A good schedule that you have created for yourself can help you avoid wasting time or getting behind in your school work. It can help you make sure that you do what you must but also have time for what you want to do.

In this unit, you will learn about two kinds of schedules: a *daily schedule* and a *weekly schedule*.

WHAT SHOULD YOU KEEP IN MIND WHEN YOU ARE CREATING A SCHEDULE?

1. Try to make each day a "balanced" one. Give yourself time each day for work and play. Include time for school work and chores at home, and for relaxation, exercise, and being with friends.

2. One part of your learning style is the time of day when you are most awake and alert. When you are most awake and alert, you can learn more efficiently. Figure out when you are most awake and alert, and make this your regular study time. Try to do your studying at this same time every day.

3. Try to spend at least some time during every school day doing school work. If you have no homework due the next day, use your regular study time for long-term assignments or reading. Make studying during your regular study time a habit. The more you get used to doing school work at that time, the easier it will be for you to study then.

4. Be sure to give yourself some free time each day. People need unplanned time to relax and unwind.

CREATING A DAILY SCHEDULE

In this exercise, you are going to create a *daily schedule* for the next school day. First, read over the directions below carefully. Then, look at the examples of daily schedules on page 99. Now, go back to direction #1 below, and, using the blank schedule on page 98, start to make your *daily schedule* for the next school day. Follow directions #1-6.

Be sure to write your schedule *in pencil,* so you can change it if you need to do so. When you have finished your schedule and are satisfied with it, you can write it over in pen if you like.

Directions:

1. Write the day of the week that is your next school day in the space provided on the schedule form.

2. Mark down the time you will wake up on this day, and when you'll go to sleep. Then, mark down the time you'll spend eating meals and being in school.

3. Next, write down your obligations — things you must do — for the day you are planning. For example: part-time job, religious school, taking care of younger children, practices, etc.

4. Now, fill in your study time(s). Pick the time(s) when you are most alert. Be sure to give yourself enough time to get your school work done well.

5. Look at the time you have left, and fill it in with other activities. Be sure to give yourself some time for things you enjoy. Also, leave yourself enough free, unplanned time.

6. Now, look at your schedule carefully. How does it seem to you? If it seems reasonable and helpful, you're finished. If not, change it so you're comfortable with it.

DAILY SCHEDULE: Day 1: _____

Time	
6:00 AM	
7:00	
8:00	
9:00	
10:00	
11:00	
12:00	
1:00 PM	
2:00	
3:00	
4:00	
5:00	
6:00	
7:00	
8:00	
9:00	
10:00	
11:00	

DAILY SCHEDULE: EXAMPLE

Day 1: _Tuesday_   Day 2: _Wednesday_

Time	Day 1 (Tuesday)	Day 2 (Wednesday)
6:00 AM		
7:00	7:15 – wake up	7:15 – wake up
8:00	breakfast; go to school	breakfast; go to school
	8:30 ↓	8:30 ↓
9:00		
10:00		
11:00		
12:00		
1:00 PM		
2:00		
3:00	FREE	Club meeting
4:00	soccer practice	
5:00	5:30 – chores; free time	5:30 – Free
6:00	6:30 – dinner	6:30 – dinner
7:00	7:30 – Free T.V.	7:30 – Free T.V.
8:00	homework	homework
9:00	9:30 ↓	9:30 ↓
10:00	T.V. Free time	
11:00	11:30 ↓ go to sleep	11:30 ↓ go to sleep

USING YOUR SCHEDULE: WHAT HAPPENED?

You now have a schedule that you've created for yourself. The next step is up to you. Try to follow your schedule for that day.

At the end of the day, take a few minutes to answer the questions below about how well your schedule worked for you.

1. How much did you follow your schedule? Circle the word or words below that best describe how much you followed your schedule.

    completely   mostly   some   a little   not at all

2. If you followed all or most of your schedule, how did you feel about using it?
   _____
   _____

3. If you didn't follow much of your schedule, what got in the way of your using it?
   _____
   _____

4. How useful did you find your schedule?
   _____
   _____

5. Do you think you will try creating another schedule? Why or why not?
   _____
   _____

CREATING A WEEKLY SCHEDULE

Some people find a daily schedule very helpful. Others find it too much trouble to be worth the effort. For some people, a *weekly schedule* can be of more value than a daily schedule.

One way to create a *weekly schedule* is to make a daily schedule for each day and put them all together. You can find printed schedule books that have a page or space for each day in most stationery stores. Usually these schedule books include all of the days in a year, with the days in each week grouped together.

Another way to make a *weekly schedule* is to list on the schedule only those events or obligations that are not part of your usual routine. When you make this kind of schedule, you assume that you already know about the things you do every day, for example, eating meals, helping at home, going to school, etc. You use the schedule to help you plan and remember special events and responsibilities, for example, studying for tests, parties, doing long-range projects, etc. You can look at an example of this kind of *weekly schedule* on page 103.

If you want to experiment with this kind of *weekly schedule,* use the schedule form on page 102. When you have followed it for a week, answer the questions about "using your schedule" on page 100 to see how it worked for you.

USING A SCHEDULE: A FEW LAST WORDS

Some people like using schedules. Others don't. Some people can benefit from writing out a schedule and following it. Other people may already plan this way in their heads.

When you consider using a schedule, the key question is this: can making and using a schedule help you do what you want and need to do? If it can, then use it. If not, then don't.

When you use a schedule, remember that it's a tool to help you, not to control you. Be flexible with it. Follow your schedule as much as you can, but recognize that you may need to change it at times.

WEEKLY SCHEDULE

	Morning	Early Afternoon	Late Afternoon	Evening
Day 1				
Day 2				
Day 3				
Day 4				
Day 5				
Day 6				
Day 7				

WEEKLY SCHEDULE

	Day 1 Sunday	Day 2 Monday	Day 3 Tuesday	Day 4 Wednesday	Day 5 Thursday	Day 6 Friday	Day 7 Saturday
Morning		Math Test				English Paper Due	Soccer Game!
Early Afternoon							
Late Afternoon		Outline English Paper		Help around the house	rewrite English Paper	Chris' Party!	
Evening	Study for Math test			Write English Paper			

UNIT XII SUMMARY: USING YOUR TIME

A *schedule* is a plan that you create for how you want to spend your time. A good schedule can help you do both what you must do and what you want to do.

When you make a schedule for yourself, keep the following ideas in mind:

1. Try to make each day a "balanced" one, giving yourself time for both work and play.

2. Figure out when you are most awake and alert, and try to do your studying then.

3. Try to spend at least some time during each school day studying. If you have no homework due the next day, work on long-term projects.

One kind of schedule is a *daily schedule*. Another kind is a *weekly schedule*.

The purpose of any schedule that you make for yourself is to help you organize your time better, so you can do what you want and need to do.